Earthquakes

Titles in the Natural Disasters series include:

Earthquakes

by Allison Lassieur

Lucent Books
San Diego, California

Library of Congress Cataloging-in-Publication Data

Lassieur, Allison.
  Earthquakes / by Allison Lassieur.
  p. cm. — (Natural disasters)
Includes bibliographical references and index.
Summary: Discusses the causes, formation, effects, and
prevention of earthquakes.
  ISBN 1-56006-975-9 (hardback : alk. paper)
  1. Earthquakes—Juvenile literature. [1. Earthquakes.]
I. Title. II. Natural disasters (Lucent Books)
  QE521.3 .L39 2002
  363.34'95—dc21

2001003359

Copyright © 2002 by Lucent Books, Inc.
10911 Technology Place, San Diego, CA 92127
Printed in the U.S.A.

Contents

Foreword

Fear and fascination are the two most common human responses to nature's most devastating events. People fear the awesome force of an earthquake, a volcanic eruption, a hurricane, and other natural phenomena with good reason. An earthquake can reduce multistory buildings to rubble in a matter of seconds. A volcanic eruption can turn lush forests and glistening lakes into a gray, flat landscape of mud and ash. A hurricane can lift houses from their foundations and hurl trucks and steel beams through the air.

As one witness to Hurricane Andrew, which hit Florida in 1992, recounts: "After the storm, planks and pieces of plywood were found impaling the trunks of large palms. . . . Eighteen-foot-long steel and concrete tie beams with roofs still attached were carried more than 150 feet. Paint was peeled from walls and street signs were sucked out of the ground and hurled through houses. Flying diesel fuel drums were a hazard, as were signs, awnings, decks, trash barrels, and fence posts that filled the skies. Mobile homes not only blew apart during the storm but disintegrated into aluminum shrapnel that became embedded in surrounding structures."

Fear is an understandable response to an event such as this but it is not the only emotion people experience when caught in the throes of a natural disaster or when news of one blares from radios or flashes across television screens. Most people are fascinated by natural forces that have the power to claim life, crush homes, tear trees from their roots, and devastate whole communities—all in an instant. Why do such terrible events as these fascinate people? Perhaps the answer lies in humanity's inability to control them, and in the knowledge that they will recur—in some cases without warning—despite the scientific community's best efforts to understand and predict them.

A great deal of scientific study has been devoted to understanding and predicting natural phenomena such as earthquakes, volcanic eruptions, and hurricanes. Geologists and seismologists monitor the earth's motion from thousands of locations around the world. Their sensitive instruments record even the slightest shifts in the large tectonic plates that make up the earth's crust. Tools such as these have greatly improved efforts to predict natural disasters. When Mt. Pinatubo in the Philippines awoke from its six-hundred-year slumber in 1991, for example, a team of scientists armed with seismometers, tiltmeters, and personal computers successfully predicted when the volcano would explode.

Clearly, the scientific community has made great strides in knowledge and in the ability to monitor and even predict some of nature's most catastrophic events. Prediction techniques have not yet been perfected, however, and control of these events eludes humanity entirely. From the moment a tropical disturbance forms over the ocean, for example, researchers can track its progress and follow every twist in its path to becoming a hurricane but they cannot predict with certainty where it will make landfall. As one researcher writes: "No one knows when or where [a catastrophic hurricane] will strike, but we do know that eventually it will blast ashore somewhere and cause massive destruction. . . . Since there is nothing anyone can do to alter that foreboding reality, the question is: Are we ready for the next great hurricane?"

The many gaps in knowledge, coupled with the inability to control these events and the certainty that they will recur, may help explain humanity's continuing fascination with natural disasters. The Natural Disasters series provides clear and careful explanations, vivid examples, and the latest information about how and why these events occur, what efforts are being made to predict them, and to prepare for them. Annotated bibliographies provide readers with ideas for further research. Fully documented primary and secondary source quotations enliven the text. Each book in this series provides students with a wealth of information as well as launching points for further study.

Introduction

The first days of January 1995 were calm and normal throughout most of Japan. The promise of a quiet year was shattered on January 17, when a devastating earthquake rocked the country. The power of the quake focused most of its destruction on the urban city of Kobe, which was the hardest hit by the quake. As *National Geographic* magazine reported later,

> The tremor lasted less than a minute. The resulting fires raged off and on for two days. The funerals went on for weeks. . . . Kobe's earthquake was the worst disaster to hit Japan since World War II. It killed 5,500 people, injured thousands more, and damaged 190,000 buildings. It toppled bridges, twisted highways, snapped ten-ton trucks like toothpicks, and severed the trunk line of Japan's famous bullet train, the technological pride of a high-tech superpower. It shut off water, gas, and electricity to nearly one million households and scrambled the underground pipes so completely that thousands of people were still without gas three months later. [1]

Not only was the loss of life devastating on that January day, but the economic loss to Japan as a result of the earthquake was staggering. As one official report commented,

> The economic loss from the 1995 earthquake may be the largest ever caused by a natural disaster in modern times. The direct damage caused by the shaking is estimated at over 147 billion dollars. [2]

Of all the natural disasters that can occur, an earthquake can be the most terrifying. It strikes without warning at any time of the day or night. The ground heaves, buildings topple, and thousands of people are killed or become homeless. An earthquake has the power to reduce major cities to rubble, inflicting millions of dollars of damage in seconds. Then, as quickly as it came, the devastating earthquake stops. The ground stops shaking, but life for the victims is changed forever.

It is estimated that today more than 75 million Americans live on or near an active earthquake fault. Millions more around the world feel the effects of earthquakes every day. In countries such as Armenia and Turkey, hundreds of thousands of people are still feeling the affects of the destructive earthquakes that shook their areas in 1988 and 1999, respectively. In the United States, large earthquakes in California and Washington State have damaged large cities in recent years and left hundreds of people homeless. No one is immune to the power of earthquakes.

Most people think of shaking ground and toppling buildings when they think of earthquakes. Although these are part of a quake, they are not the only destructive forces at work. Landslides, ground subsidence, and enormous sea waves called tsunamis sometimes injure or kill thousands more than the earthquake itself. Earthquakes and their effects can reduce a vibrant city to rubble in seconds.

The power of an earthquake can reduce a seemingly sound building to rubble.

Nothing was left standing after a tsunami hit this town in Chile.

In centuries past, no one understood earthquakes. People attributed the shaking of the ground to gods, spirits, and other supernatural beliefs. As science replaced myth, new information about earthquakes and the structure of the earth came to light. People no longer ascribed the shaking earth to angry gods or supernatural beasts. Instead, they began to understand that earthquakes were a part of the natural forces that have shaped the earth for thousands of years. The world's majestic mountain ranges are created by the same forces that create earthquakes, for example. The landslides that accompany earthquakes change the landscape, creating new features while destroying the old. When the earth moves, nothing stays the same.

Earthquakes in History

The North American continent in 1811 was a wild and unknown land. The pioneer movement that would soon grip the United States had not yet taken hold, and vast areas of the country were still wilderness. Missouri was part of that wilderness, and the town of New Madrid, a small river town about 180 miles south of St. Louis, was little more than a village nestled comfortably at the edge of the civilized world.

There was nothing extraordinary about New Madrid. That is, not until the evening of December 16, 1811. That night the townspeople, looking forward to their Christmas celebrations, had gone to

The Missouri town of New Madrid, was the epicenter of a series of large earthquakes in 1811 and 1812 that were felt hundreds of miles away.

bed. Suddenly, around 2 A.M., the ground began to shake. One anonymous resident of the town later wrote a description of what happened for the local newspaper:

> About 2 o'clock this morning we were awakened by a most tremendous noise, which the house danced about and seemed as if it would fall on our heads. I soon conjectured the cause of our troubles, and cried out it was an Earthquake, and for the family to leave the house; which we found very difficult to do, owing to its rolling and jostling about. . . . At the time of this shock, the heavens were very clear and serene, not a breath of air stirring; but in five minutes it became very dark, and a vapour which seemed to impregnate the atmosphere, had a disagreeable smell, and produced a difficulty of respiration. . . . The darkness continued until daybreak; during this time we had eight more shocks, none of them so violent as the first. . . . At half past 6 o'clock in the morning it cleared up, and believing the danger over I left home. . . . A few minutes after my departure there was another shock, extremely violent. I hurried home as fast as I could, but the agitation of the Earth was so great that it was with much difficulty I kept my balance—the motion of the Earth was about 12 inches to and fro. I cannot give you an accurate description of this moment; the Earth seemed convulsed—the houses shook very much—chimneys falling in every direction. The loud, hoarse roaring which attended the earthquake, together with the cries, screams, and yells of the people, seems still ringing in my ears. [3]

The earthquake that woke New Madrid citizens on that December morning was only the first in a series of powerful shocks. The second shock occurred on January 23, 1812, at about 9 A.M. The third shock, which some modern scientists think was the most powerful, was recorded on February 7, 1812, at about 3:45 A.M. The shocks that shook New Madrid affected a huge area, including Arkansas, southeastern Missouri, western Tennessee, and western Kentucky. Although the earthquakes were felt for miles around, they became known as the New Madrid quakes.

New Madrid Earthquakes Felt for Miles

After the first three major earthquakes, the area was shaken by more than two hundred aftershocks in the following weeks. The sparsely populated areas surrounding New Madrid were not the only places affected by these earthquakes. Some of the shocks were so powerful that they were noted in almost every major city on the East Coast. People in Washington, D.C., New Orleans, and Quebec City felt the tremors. As author Philip Fradkin notes,

> The shocks appeared in historical accounts in twenty-seven states. A Michigan judge later journeyed into northern Canada and wrote that residents there had experienced nine shocks, the same number he had tallied in his home state. The earthquakes were felt in Boston, New York, . . . Charleston, . . . and New Orleans, just to name a few places. . . . Flashes of light were observed in Savannah, Georgia, and low, rumbling noises were heard as far away as Washington, D.C.[4]

President James Madison (pictured) wrote an account of the New Madrid earthquake in a letter to his friend, Thomas Jefferson.

In the nation's capital, President James Madison included a comment about the earthquakes in a letter to his friend and predecessor Thomas Jefferson. He wrote,

> The reiteration of Earthquakes continues to be reported from various quarters. They have slightly reached the State of N.Y. and been severely felt W. [west] and S. [south] Westwardly. There was one here this morning at 5 or 6 minutes after 4

o'C[lock]. It was rather stronger than any preceding one, and lasted several minutes; with sensible tho' very slight repetitions throughout the succeeding hour.[5]

Although New Madrid managed to survive the first two earthquakes, the last major quake in February completely destroyed the town. Buildings that had remained standing collapsed. Townspeople fled the area, and the roads were filled with the homeless. The most dramatic effect of the February shock, however, was on the Mississippi River. The riverbed was lifted near New Madrid, reversing the flow of the mighty river. Waterfalls were created where none had been before. The earthquake also caused the formation of Reelfoot Lake in upper northwestern Tennessee. Authors Kerry Sieh and Simon LeVay describe how the earthquake created the lake: "The Reelfoot River, a small tributary that joins the Mississippi near New Madrid, was blocked by uplift of a portion of its bed, causing an 18-mile long body of water to collect on the sunken land upstream and to the northeast. Reelfoot Lake persists to this day."[6]

Reelfoot Lake was created by the New Madrid earthquake.

Robert Mallet: Early Seismologist

In the 1800s most people still believed that earthquakes were caused by gods or other supernatural events. One person who did not believe such stories was Robert Mallet. Most seismologists consider Mallet the first person to seriously study earthquakes as a scientific phenomenon.

Mallet was born in Ireland in 1810. He became a gifted engineer who designed railroad stations, bridges, and other large structures. He also had a strong interest in learning more about earthquakes and how they affected structures.

Mallet collected and studied thousands of books, newspaper articles, and other writings about earthquakes. From this information he created one of the first earthquake catalogs. The catalogs listed more than six thousand earthquakes, their locations, and their effects. Later seismologists used Mallet's catalog to create the first reliable seismic maps of the world.

Mallet was also one of the first to experiment with artificial earthquakes. He exploded dynamite underground then measured the energy waves that came from the explosion. He learned that earthquake waves travel at different speeds through different materials.

By the time of his death in 1881, Robert Mallet had significantly contributed to the study of earthquakes.

Origin of New Madrid Earthquakes a Mystery

At the time of the New Madrid earthquakes, this type of natural disaster was scarcely heard of in North America. Scientists of the time had no real idea about why or how earthquakes occurred. Many theories were proposed, and many people believed that earthquakes had something to do with electricity, which was generally considered to be a magical force. The St. Louis *Gazette* newspaper summarized prevailing ideas for its nineteenth-century readers:

According to the hypothesis of some, earthquakes are occasioned [caused] by subterranean fires throwing down the arches or vaults of the Earth; according to others the [earthquakes are caused by] rarefaction of the abyss waters, interior combustion and fermentation, volcanic operations, and lately by the electric fluid. The latter hypothesis seems to be most accredited, as it is evidently the most rational. The instantaneous effects of the earthquakes prove beyond a doubt that electricity is the principal agent in this alarming and terrible phenomenon.[7]

The New Madrid earthquakes were the talk of the nation for a few weeks, as people around the country struggled to understand what had happened. Slowly, however, the aftershocks trailed off. Since the most affected areas of the country were rural and isolated, the country gradually lost interest in such faraway news. Soon other events, such as the War of 1812, pushed the earthquakes from the minds of many people.

People Disbelieve the Destruction

Not only did current events overshadow the New Madrid earthquakes, but also many people simply refused to believe that the earthquakes had been as deadly as was reported. The areas where the earthquakes hit were remote, and few people actually traveled there to see the effects of the disaster. Even scientists and geologists were skeptical that the New Madrid earthquakes were significant. In the face of such disbelief, memories of the quakes quickly faded. As the years passed, fewer people believed that the earthquakes had even happened. In 1883 one scientist wrote a paper entitled "The 'Earthquake' at New Madrid, Missouri in 1811, Probably Not an Earthquake."

In later years, scientists realized how significant the New Madrid earthquakes were. Today, geologists suspect that the three main shocks were some of the largest earthquakes ever to hit the United States. But just as the scientists of New Madrid were unable to determine why or how the earthquakes happened, scientists around the world have also struggled to explain the origins of earthquakes.

Earthquakes Felt Throughout the World

Earthquakes have always been a worldwide phenomenon. Earthquakes have been recorded for centuries on almost every continent. One of the most complete records of earthquake activity is in China, where writings that mention earthquakes date back several centuries to the Shang dynasty. The oldest recorded earthquake occurred in the Shandong Province of China in 1831 B.C. The record notes that Tai Shan Mountain shook. Later accounts are much more detailed, and China has more complete records dating from about 780 B.C. These records are so specific that scholars have been able to piece together a clear picture of ancient Chinese earthquakes. As scientist Bruce A. Bolt says,

Records of earthquakes in China date back as far as 1831 B.C. Shown are buildings in the Chinese city of Lijiang after an earthquake in 1996.

Predicting Earthquakes in Ancient China

China has been rocked by earthquakes for tens of centuries. In A.D. 132, Chinese scholar Chang Heng invented the first seismoscope, a device that could detect earthquakes. The seismoscope that Chang built was shaped like a large jar. The vessel, made of copper, measured about three feet in diameter and eight feet tall. It was elaborately decorated with carvings of animals, including eight fierce dragons. Each dragon head faced outward along the rim of the vessel, and each held a ball in its mouth. Squatting below the dragons were eight open-mouthed metal frogs, positioned to catch a ball in case one dropped.

Chang told people that if an earthquake occurred, the shaking would dislodge a ball from the mouth of one of the dragons, signaling from which direction the earthquake came.

Few Chinese believed the device would work. Then one day a ball dropped. No one had felt an earthquake, but Chang insisted that an earthquake had occurred somewhere to the west, in the direction that dragon was pointing. Sure enough, ten days later a messenger arrived with the news that an earthquake had hit a village to the west. As a result of his miraculous prediction, Chang became a respected scientist.

Was his prediction luck, or science? Today, most scientists think that Chang had a very lucky day. While seismologists suspect that the mechanics of the device were similar to a modern seismograph, no one knows for sure. Most scientists agree that Chang's device probably would not have been sensitive enough to detect a quake at a distance. The internal structure of the earthquake-prediction machine was never recorded, and how the machine worked remains a mystery.

Modern studies have been able to establish the distribution of damage and hence, the size of the earthquakes. For example, the San-ho earthquake of September 2, 1679, the greatest known near Beijing, was mentioned in the records of 121 cities. When modern researchers compared the descriptions of building damage, ground cracks, and other geological features near the source, together with reports of shaking from distant places, with earthquakes of recent times, they concluded that its size was similar to that of the San Francisco earthquake of 1906. [8]

China is not the only country to record severe earthquakes in its ancient history. Ancient Rome and Greece were constantly plagued by tremors. Ancient religious writings, including the Bible, include references to earthquakes. Some scholars and scientists believe that biblical events such as the parting of the Red Sea and the falling of the walls of Jericho may have been caused by earthquakes.

Earthquakes were recorded in many areas during the Middle Ages and Renaissance. In the 1500s, England was hit with earthquakes that a young William Shakespeare certainly must have experienced. Quebec Province in Canada was rocked by a huge earthquake in 1663, which was recorded by Jesuit priests in the area. Earthquakes have been common in Central and South America, as well as in Russia and Japan. Many parts of Europe, including Turkey, Greece, Italy, Spain, Portugal, and Germany, have been shaken by earthquakes.

Some scholars believe that the parting of the Red Sea as depicted in the Bible may have been caused by an earthquake.

The United States has also had its share of earthquakes. An earthquake damaged Boston in 1775, just one year before the colonists declared independence from Britain. One Boston citizen wrote a letter describing the experience, saying,

On the 18th Instant about 25 minutes past four in the morning a very severe shock of an earthquake was felt in this Town and I suppose all over New England. A great part of the Houses in the Town were damag'd, many chimneys thrown down, and roofs beat in with the fall of the Bricks; but thro' the mercy of God, no Man's Life lost: It is esteem'd the severest shock by far that was ever felt in New England.[9]

In August 1886 a massive earthquake shook Charleston, South Carolina. Many of the brick buildings in town collapsed, and about sixty people were killed. One man who was staying in the Charleston Hotel at the time the earthquake hit wrote a description of his attempt to flee a crumbling brick building:

> At the very first shock the lights in the house all went out, and I was in perfect darkness. Then the plastering began to fall. It flashed through my mind that I should endeavor to get out of the house, and I got out into the corridor and groped my way, in utter darkness, amid falling plaster. . . . When I reached the ground floor . . . the air was filled with plaster dust. All around was a terrible roaring and moaning sound, and the din [a loud noise] was heightened by the falling of timbers. I found the front door of the house closed, a fortunate thing for me, as it saved my life. It took me a moment to find the knob, and as I was looking for it tons of brick fell down from the upper part of the house in front of the door. If I had found the door open I would have been buried under the bricks. I ran out through the heaps of fallen bricks and fell twice in getting to the middle of the street. There I remained terror-stricken.[10]

Supernatural Explanations of Earthquakes

Although earthquakes have occurred throughout history, until relatively recently no one understood how or why they happened. Many religions taught that a deity controlled the motions of the earth, and almost every culture throughout the world developed elaborate stories and mythologies to explain the periodic appearance of the deadly tremors. The ancient Greeks believed earthquakes were caused by angry gods. In Greek mythology, Poseidon, ruler of the sea, caused great earthquakes when he was angry. The Roman god Neptune not only caused earthquakes, but he could also make the oceans rise into terrible waves that flooded the land. Mexican legends told that *El Diablo* (the devil) made a huge rip in the ground so he could easily travel to the earth. The Hindus of India believed that the world was held up by elephants. When an elephant became tired, it shook its head, which caused earthquakes. Russian tales described a god named Tuli who drove a sled that carried the earth. The sled was pulled by flea-infested dogs. When one dog stopped to scratch a flea, the whole earth shook. The Chinese thought that a giant frog carried the earth, and earthquakes occurred when the frog twitched.

One of the most colorful earthquake legends comes from Japan, where the people believed that a giant catfish lived in the mud beneath the earth. As one scholar relates,

> The catfish liked to play pranks and could only be restrained by Kashima, a god who protected the Japanese people from earthquakes. So long as Kashima kept a mighty rock with magical powers over the catfish, the earth was still. But when he relaxed his guard, the catfish thrashed about, causing earthquakes.[11]

According to ancient Greek myth, Poseidon, the god of the sea, caused great earthquakes when he was angry.

Some Native American tribes have traditional stories about earthquakes. Many of these stories are part of the creation legends of the tribes, such as this American Indian story from southern California:

> Long ago, when most of the world was water, Great Spirit decided to make a beautiful land with lakes and rivers, that six turtles carried on their backs. One day the turtles began

to argue and three of the turtles began to swim east, while the other three swam west. The earth shook! It cracked with a loud noise. The turtles could not swim far, because the land on their backs was heavy. When they saw they could not swim far away they stopped arguing and made up. But every once in a while, the turtles that hold up California argue again, and each time they do, the earth shakes.[12]

First Attempts at Scientific Explanations

Although most people in ancient times ascribed earthquakes to supernatural forces, a few early scientists attempted to explain earthquakes in other ways. One of the earliest scholars to study earthquakes was the Greek writer Thales. His main interest was the study of the oceans, and he theorized that the earth floated on the waters of the seas. He explained earthquakes by suggesting that the movement of the ocean waves caused the earth to shake.

Another ancient scholar, Anaximenes, theorized that falling rocks inside the earth hit other rocks, causing them to vibrate in a way that produced house-shaking earthquakes.

Aristotle believed that earthquakes were caused by subterranean fires that burned away supports for earth's outer parts.

One of the most influential scientists of the ancient world was the great scholar Aristotle. He also had a theory about earthquakes. Aristotle, who was born about 250 years after Thales, in 384 B.C., observed many natural phenomena, such as thunder, lightning, and fire. He used his observations to devise an explanation for earthquakes. As writer Bruce A. Bolt explains,

Aristotle was convinced that there existed "a central fire" inside the Earth, although Greek thinkers differed as to its cause. Aristotle's theory held that caverns underground would produce fire in the same way as storm clouds produce lightning. This fire would rise rapidly and, if obstructed, would burst violently through the surrounding rocks, causing vibrations and noise. . . . Subterranean fires would burn away the supports of the outer parts of the Earth. The ensuing collapse of the cavern roofs would create the shocks experienced as earthquakes. Aristotle's linking of subterranean and atmospheric events and his view that dry and smoky vapors cause earthquakes under the Earth, although incorrect, were widely accepted until the eighteenth century. [13]

Not only did Aristotle put forth a scientific explanation for earthquakes, he set up classifications of quakes according to whether they were accompanied by "escape of vapors. [In his treatise called] *Meteoralogica*, . . . he explained a wide variety of natural phenomena . . . [he wrote,] 'Places whose subsoil is poor are shaken more because of the large amount of wind they absorb.' " [14]

Aristotle was also one of the first scientists to associate the weather with earthquakes. He reasoned that earthquake weather existed—atmospheric conditions that were favorable for a quake. He believed that air was drawn inside the earth before an earthquake, making the air above the earth thinner and harder to breathe. His ideas were echoed more than four hundred years later by the scholar Pliny, who wrote, "Tremors of the earth never occur except when the sea is 'calm and the sky so still that birds are unable to soar because all the breath that carries them has been withdrawn." [15]

Today, many of these ancient ideas seem primitive. But these intellectuals were among the first who tried to explain earthquakes with science instead of myth and superstition. Their theories, although incorrect, do include a number of points that are true about earthquakes. As Aristotle suggested, earthquakes are triggered by movements in the earth, and indeed, structures on loose soil tend to sustain more than average damage during an earthquake. Also, his association of "vapors" with earthquake activity might have been an attempt to account for the gases such as sulfur that are sometimes released during an earthquake. Even though many of his ideas were later proven wrong, Aristotle did make a significant contribution to the early understanding of earthquakes.

Science Replaces Mythology

Physical laws formulated by Sir Isaac Newton would later be used to explain earthquakes.

Although a few thinkers, such as Aristotle, tried to understand earthquakes by applying scientific principles to observed phenomena, even educated people continued to believe the myths and superstitions. Not until the eighteenth century—the Age of Enlightenment—did science begin to replace religion in explaining natural phenomena. One of the most influential scientists of this time was Sir Isaac Newton. In 1687 he published the work known as *Principia Mathematica*, considered by some to be one of the greatest scientific writings of all time. Significantly, it set forth many scientific formulas that would later be used to explain earthquakes. According to author Bolt,

> Newton's *Principia Mathematica* at last provided a formulation capable of unifying all terrestrial motions, including earthquakes. His laws of motion provided the physical theory needed to explain earthquake waves, and his law of gravitation provided the basis for understanding the geological forces that shape the Earth.[16]

Newton's ideas encouraged scientists to observe and record geological changes and to consider how those changes might be linked to earthquakes. Author Bolt explains,

> By the middle of the eighteenth century, scientists and engineers under the influence of Newtonian mechanics began to publish memoirs that associated earthquakes with waves traveling through rocks in the Earth. These memoirs gave a

great deal of attention to the geological effects of earthquakes, including landslides, ground movements, changes of sea level, and damage to buildings. For example, some observers noted, as the Greeks had, that structures on soft ground were usually more damaged by earthquakes than those on hard ground.[17]

The scientists of the Age of Enlightenment made great strides in understanding earthquakes, but their ideas were mainly theoretical. The technology to accurately measure nature's physical forces did not yet exist. Because they lacked factual information, their ideas were largely ignored by the public. Old beliefs that earthquakes were caused by divine intervention or mythological events continued to hold sway. It would be another two hundred years before new advances in science and technology would unlock the secrets of earthquakes.

What Causes Earthquakes?

No one living in the bustling city of San Francisco in early 1906 could have imagined the horror that was to befall them on the morning of April 18. At 5:12 A.M., a massive earthquake struck the large, sleeping city. This quake, which became known as the San Francisco earthquake, destroyed much of the city and ushered in a new era of earthquake study.

But the residents of San Francisco did not know that this earthquake would revolutionize science. To them, the world was ending. Author John H. Hodgson described the powerful and deadly events of that morning:

> They [the people] were awakened by the most violent shaking imaginable—"like a terrier shaking a rat"—and by the frightful roar caused by the writhing and collapse of buildings. Over all this was the insane clanging of church bells as the belfries swayed in the violence of the motion. Some people didn't hear the clanging. They were killed by the collapse of their own houses, or by their chimneys crashing through their roofs to crush them in their beds. People on the streets had an equally terrifying experience. Everywhere the shaking was violent . . . [and] the earth appeared to be thrown into waves which broke the pavement into great cracks and twisted tram-rails as if they had been putty.[18]

The powerful earthquake did not spare people in the countryside, either. As authors Kerry Sieh and Simon LeVay relate,

Many agricultural workers were already in the fields; some of them heard a rumbling sound, and then by the gray predawn light, they saw waves riding along the ground as if it had suddenly been transformed into a windswept sea. Some trees were shaken so severely that their crowns touched the ground, and the trunks of others snapped off entirely. . . . Water tanks overturned, and the ground itself failed in many places, torn by landslides, fissures, and sand-blows [a hole in the earth from which sand and dirt explodes]. Railroad lines buckled and water pipes broke, sometimes in hundreds of places.[19]

Sailors at sea felt the shocks, and some believed they had run aground even though they were safely in deep water. The chief engineer of one steamship described his experience: "The ship

On the morning of April 18, 1906, a massive earthquake struck San Francisco, leveling many buildings in the city.

seemed to jump out of the water; the engines raced fearfully, as though the shaft or wheel had gone; then came a violent trembling fore and aft sideways, like running at full speed against a wall of ice."[20]

San Francisco Goes Up in Flames

The earthquake was only the beginning of the terror. Soon after the shaking stopped, the survivors were stunned by another disaster: fire. In less than half an hour, more than fifty fires broke out in different parts of the city. It was not long before the fires raged out of control. Worse, there was no water to fight the blazes. The fires raged for three days and completely destroyed the city. According to Sieh and LeVay,

A total of 28,188 buildings were destroyed in an area of 4.1 square miles. According to the Army's body count, 498 persons died in the earthquake or the fire; about four times as

Within half an hour following the onset of the 1906 San Francisco earthquake, more than fifty fires broke out, completely destroying the city.

Discovering the Real Cause of Earthquakes

In the 1800s the science of geology was just beginning. One of the most respected scientists in the field was an adventurer named Grove Karl Gilbert. His lifelong passion for earth study took him throughout the United States, and he eventually became one of the six founding geologists of the U.S. Geological Survey in 1879. But his most significant claim to earthquake fame came in 1906, when he studied the effects of the San Francisco earthquake.

Gilbert was sleeping at the University of California, Berkeley, when he was awakened by the quake. His excitement at experiencing an earthquake is clear from a passage he wrote later quoted in Philip Fradkin's book, *Magnitude 8:*

> It is the natural and legitimate ambition of a properly constituted geologist to see a glacier, witness [a volcanic] eruption and feel an earthquake. The glacier is always ready, awaiting his visit; the eruption has a course to run, . . . but the earthquake, unheralded and brief, may elude him through his entire lifetime. . . . When, therefore, I was awakened in Berkeley on the eighteenth day of April last by a tumult of motions and noises, it was with unalloyed pleasure that I became aware that a vigorous earthquake was in progress.

In the weeks following the devastating quake, Gilbert studied the land around the San Francisco area. He had one advantage that other scientists had never had: The city and surrounding areas had been thoroughly surveyed in prior years, giving Gilbert accurate measurements of the land and geological formations before the earthquake. When he compared measurements he took after the earthquake to the old ones, he was surprised to find that some areas had shifted significantly.

What he eventually discovered was that the earthquake had been caused by a huge fault, or rupture, in the land beneath San Francisco. This discovery gave geologists their first set of fresh evidence of the severe earth movements that occurred during an earthquake. It proved beyond a doubt that earthquakes were somehow connected with cataclysmic shifts in the earth.

many were unaccounted for and probably also died. Property losses were $450 million in 1906 dollars (about $7 billion in current dollars). [21]

The San Francisco earthquake and fire became one of the deadliest and costliest natural disasters in U.S. history. However, no one knew how or why the immense earthquake had occurred. Thus the question of the origin of earthquakes was hotly debated by everyone from professors to philosophers to theologians to families around the kitchen table. Everyone had an opinion, and the opinion of many remained that supernatural or magical forces were responsible for earthquakes. Some, however, sought a scientific explanation.

The San Francisco earthquake offered a prime opportunity to collect and analyze firsthand scientific data about earthquakes and their causes. One scientist, Grove Karl Gilbert, was in San Francisco during the quake and studied the area in the weeks after the shock. He realized that the earthquake had been caused by a huge fault, or crack, in the land beneath San Francisco.

However, geology, the study of the history of the earth, and seismology, the study of earthquakes, were infant sciences in 1906. It would be more than fifty years before the mystery would be completely solved. It would be part of a larger study about how the earth was formed, called plate tectonics.

Continental Drift

Long before San Francisco was rocked by the great quake, science had struggled with explanations about the world and the forces that shape it. During the Age of Exploration, which began in the 1400s, travelers and explorers began to map the world. These maps showed the outlines of the continents for the first time. Many cartographers (mapmakers) and scholars realized that the continents were shaped like puzzle pieces that would fit together if pushed toward each other. They began to wonder if this meant that the continents were once part of a single land mass. This idea was first suggested by Dutch mapmaker Abraham Oertel in 1596. In his book, *Thesaurus Geographicus*, he says that the Americas were "torn away from Europe and Africa . . . by earthquakes and floods. . . . The vestiges [remains] of the rupture reveal themselves, if someone brings forward a map of the world and considers carefully the coasts of the three [continents]."[22]

Oertel's idea was ignored for centuries. Then in 1912 German scientist Alfred Lothar Wegener surprised the scientific community with his theory of continental drift. He pointed out, as Oertel had done, that some of the earth's land masses looked like puzzle pieces that fit together. As authors Sieh and LeVay explain,

> Most strikingly, the long, winding "S" shape formed by the Atlantic seaboards of Greenland, North America, and South America could fit fairly snugly against the corresponding western seaboards of Europe and Africa. The fit is even better if one matches not the shorelines but the margins of the continental shelves—the strips of relatively shallow water—that extend variable distances from the coasts of the Atlantic Ocean.[23]

Wegener called this huge land mass Pangaea, which means "all land." He believed that Pangaea split apart about 200 million years ago, forming the continents of the earth as we see them today.

Wegener did not look at only the land masses to support his theory. He also used facts from geology, biology, and climatology—the study of weather patterns. For example, if North America and Europe are lined up, the Appalachian Mountains in the eastern United States line up with the Grampian Mountains in Scotland. Also, Wegener noted that many fossils of the same dinosaur species and other extinct creatures had turned up in different

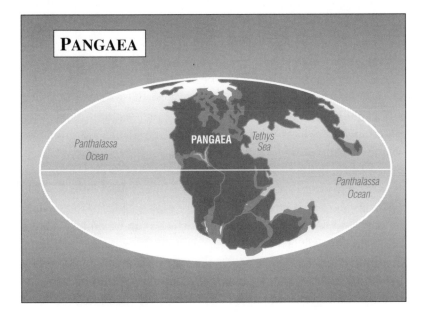

PANGAEA

Panthalassa Ocean

PANGAEA

Tethys Sea

Panthalassa Ocean

places all over the world, suggesting that the landmasses of the planet had once been connected.

The greatest flaw in Wegener's theory was the lack of an explanation for how the great landmasses could have moved. It seemed inconceivable that such huge areas could break away from one another and later arrive at distant positions. Most scientists argued that the continents do not float in the oceans and they were stationary in the places where they were created.

In the 1950s the scientific community took interest in Wegener's continental drift theory. During that time, new advances in technology enabled scientists to study the earth's surface more closely. In the 1950s scientists had begun using sonar equipment to map the ocean floor. To their amazement, they discovered massive undersea mountain ranges and deep trenches. They also found that rocks in some areas of the ocean bottom were younger than others, suggesting that new landmasses had been formed and had moved over the centuries. One scientist, Princeton geology professor Harry Hess, offered a dramatic explanation, suggesting "that the ridges and trenches were, in effect, the on- and off-ramps of vast conveyor belts that carried large pieces of crust across Earth's surface."[24]

In Hess's theory, ongoing volcanic action at the ridges created new crust, and the rock on the "off-ramp" moved away from the ridges until it reached a trench, a deep area into which it sank.

Plate Tectonics Explains Earthquakes

Geologists were excited at the new idea because it explained a great deal about worldwide earthquake activity. One final piece to the puzzle of earthquakes remained, however, and it was proposed by Canadian geophysicist J. Tuzo Wilson. He theorized that the earth's surface was divided into a number of large plates. He called his idea plate tectonics.

According to the plate tectonics theory, the earth's crust is made up of about twelve enormous slabs, or plates, that are in constant motion. Miles beneath the earth's surface is the mantle—a layer of hot liquid rock. The plates float on top of the mantle like rafts, constantly moved and pushed by the heat from the earth. They move at speeds from less than one centimeter to about ten centimeters every year, which is about as fast as fingernails grow.

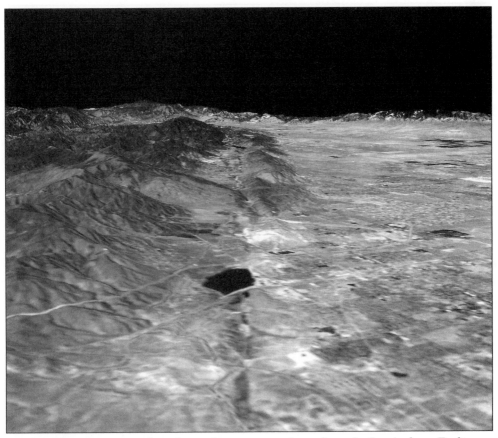

Most earthquakes occur where large plates meet, such as along the San Andreas Fault (pictured).

Finally, geologists who studied earthquakes had the answer they were looking for: the reason why the earth moved. As a result of understanding plate tectonics, scientists now know that contrary to earlier beliefs, earthquakes do not occur randomly on the earth's surface. Most earthquakes follow the long lines where large plates meet. For example, the San Andreas Fault lies along the boundaries of the Pacific plate and the North American plate. Japan, which is plagued by earthquakes, is located in an area where four plates grind together: the North American plate, the Eurasian plate, the Pacific plate, and the Philippine Sea plate.

Scientists also looked at maps of earthquake activity throughout the world and saw that a majority of earthquakes occur in a belt of

seismic and volcanic activity known as the Ring of Fire. This band follows the boundaries of a number of plates, stretching for thousands of miles around the floor of the Pacific Ocean. The plate tectonics theory was instrumental in finally explaining earthquakes.

Earthquakes Occur at Plate Boundaries

Today's geologists know that earthquakes occur in response to motion of the tectonic plates at plate boundaries. Some earthquakes occur over spreading zones, where two plates move away from each other. Other earthquakes originate in trenches, where two plates collide. Still others result from movement at transform faults, where two plates slide sideways against each other. The San Andreas Fault is one of the most dramatic transform faults, but many others are scattered throughout the world.

Faults and Earthquakes

As geologists used this new information to study earthquakes, they realized that many quakes occur near faults—a crack or rupture in a rock formation. As Bolt explains, "Most people . . . have observed abrupt changes in structure of the rocks. In some places one type of rock can be seen butting up against rock of quite another type along a narrow line of contact."[25]

Elsewhere, layers of the same rock have been displaced, either vertically or horizontally. These displacements are called faults. Faults can be short and only a few feet, but large ruptures may measure hundreds of miles. Not all faults appear on the earth's surface as offset layers of rock. Some form deep beneath the ground as a result of pressure at plate boundaries. Generally speaking, the larger the rupture, the stronger the earthquake.

The San Andreas Fault is a dramatic example of a transform fault, where two plates slide sideways against each other.

The two main types of faults are inactive and active. Most faults are inactive, which means that no significant earthquake activity has been recorded there. The last movement along an inactive fault may have occurred millions of years ago.

The faults where earthquakes occur are known as active faults. Geologists use certain clues in the topography of the earth to determine if a fault is active. Fresh scarps—steep exposed walls of rock that thrust up from the ground—are one clue. Scarps can be as small as a few inches or as large as several feet. Scientists also look at erosion and sedimentary deposits to determine when the area moved. Buried leaves and twigs, along with other organic material, decay at known rates and can also give information about when a fault might have been active.

Types of Faults

Although a fault is a rupture in the earth, all faults are not the same. Normal faults occur when the rock is pulled or is under tension. Reverse faults happen when the rock is squeezed or compressed. Both normal and reverse faults can create another kind

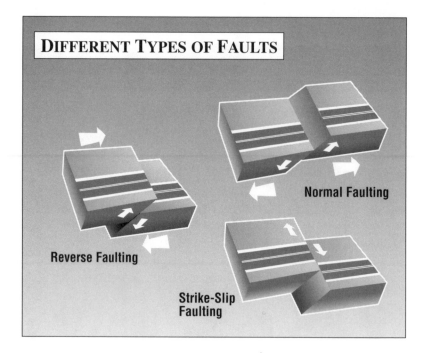

DIFFERENT TYPES OF FAULTS

Normal Faulting

Reverse Faulting

Strike-Slip Faulting

of fault, a strike-slip fault. In a strike-slip fault, the sections of rock are either pushed or pulled, and they move horizontally past one another. Sometimes earthquakes can occur far away from active faults, fault lines, and plate boundaries. Scientists call these intraplate quakes, and they are still unclear why these earthquakes occur. Some speculate that plate movements might put pressure on old faults far beneath the earth's surface. The New Madrid earthquake, for example, was a famous intraplate earthquake.

Elastic Rebound

Regardless of the type of fault that produces an earthquake or where it occurs, an earthquake is the vibration of the earth's surface that follows a release of energy. With the passage of time, the two sides of the fault push at or pull against each other, constantly creating energy. Sometimes the two sides stick together, and they are unable to move. They might remain stuck together for centuries. Suddenly the two sides pop apart with great force, like a rubber band that is stretched and released. Scientists call this elastic rebound.

According to the theory, over time, as the plates move against one another, forces deep beneath the crust deform the rocks. This deformation is called elastic strain. As the rocks strain, they change shape. Finally, at the weakest area of the strained rock, a sudden slip occurs. The rocks spring, or rebound, to their original shapes, causing an enormous amount of energy to be released. The waves of energy that are released from the rebound cause earthquakes, and the amount of energy that is released determines the strength of the quake. As Bolt describes,

> This elastic rebound has been confirmed over the years since 1906 to be the immediate cause of tectonic earthquakes. Like a watch spring that is wound tighter and tighter, the more that rocks are elastically strained, the more energy they store. When a fault ruptures, the elastic energy stored in the rocks is released quickly, partly as heat and partly as elastic waves. These waves constitute the earthquake.[26]

Other Causes of Earthquakes

Today, most scientists believe that a majority of quakes are caused by elastic rebound and fault slippage. However, earthquakes can be triggered by other forces in the earth. Volcanic activity is one of the main triggers of earthquakes in some areas, and the quakes that result are called volcanic earthquakes. Volcanic earthquakes are caused when hot magma deep beneath a volcano begins to move. As the magma moves, it pushes the surrounding rocks, creating strain and causing the rocks to become hot. Finally, the pressure produces so much strain on the rocks that they break, causing a release of energy that becomes an earthquake.

Seismologists and volcanologists monitor volcanic earthquakes and their effects to help predict when a volcano will erupt. In most cases, strong volcanic earthquakes rock an area in the weeks and months before a volcanic eruption. In the massive 1835 Cosigüina volcanic eruption in Nicaragua, for example, earthquakes rocked the area before and during the blast:

> About 3 P.M. earthquakes described as "undulations of the earth" rocked the whole area. . . . Many men, who were walking in a . . . procession, were thrown down. The darkness lasted forty-three hours, making it indispensable for everyone to carry a light, and even with their aid, it was impossible to see clearly. [27]

Another earthquake trigger is water. In many places around the world, earthquakes have been created by the filling of large reservoirs. One of the most famous examples of this kind of earthquake happened in the United States in the 1930s. When the Hoover Dam was built along the Colorado River, it formed Lake Mead. The area had never recorded any earthquake activity, but as engineers started releasing water to fill the lake, earthquakes began to shake the area. The earthquakes continued throughout the time the lake filled, and residents are still shaken by periodic earthquakes. Fortunately, the earthquakes are minor and very little damage occurs.

Although the cause of water-created earthquakes is an enigma, geologists have offered a few theories as to why quakes are triggered by reservoirs. Authors James M. Gere and Haresh C. Shah listed these theories:

When Hoover Dam was built to create a reservoir, the movement of the water to fill the lake created earthquakes in the area.

First, the weight of the water places a load on the earth, creating stresses in the underlying soil and rock. Second, these additional stresses cause an increase in pressure in the parts of the soil and rock that contained water before the filling of the reservoir took place. And third, water from the reservoir flows into the underlying material, increasing its water content and filling cracks and pores. Any or all of these effects can result in earthquakes.[28]

Throughout history, scientists had struggled to explain earthquakes. Over the years, supernatural explanations were replaced by fact as geologists uncovered clues to the cause of earthquakes. With the acceptance of the continental drift and plate tectonics theories, many mysteries of earthquakes were solved. Today, scientists understand how earthquakes occur and where they are most likely to strike.

The Earth Moves

Good Friday, March 27, 1964, was fairly unremarkable for the residents of Anchorage, Alaska. Most people were looking forward to a quiet spring holiday that late afternoon when the earth began to shake. It was one of the most powerful earthquakes of the twentieth century, and for four minutes enormous tremors rocked the city.

Geologist John R. Williams, who was relaxing in his apartment in Anchorage when the earthquake began, provides this account:

In 1964, one of the most powerful earthquakes of the twentieth century hit Anchorage, Alaska, destroying much of the city, including this school.

At first we noticed a rattling of the building. The initial shaking lasted perhaps five to ten seconds. The first shaking was followed without any noticeable quiet period by a strong rolling motion which appeared to move from east to west. After a few seconds of the strong rolling motion, I took my son to the door leading to the hall, opened the door to prevent jamming, and stood in the doorway. I looked in the hallway and back in the apartment and noticed blocks working against one another in interior walls and saw some fall into the street and into the apartment hall. I took my son and ran to a parked car. I looked at the building, which was swaying in an east-west direction. Blocks were toppling, ground heaving, trees and poles were swaying strongly. The Hillside apartment building was a total loss.[29]

This account of an earthquake in action clearly describes the devastation that happens when a quake strikes. Buildings and structures are damaged, the ground moves, and falling debris threatens to injure or kill. People who have experienced earthquakes throughout history have experienced these effects, but until the middle of the twentieth century, science had no explanation as to why earthquakes behave as they do. Today, scientists and geologists have a much more complete picture of what happens when the earth moves.

What Happens During an Earthquake

Over the years, geologists have studied records from past earthquakes and observed the effects of recent disasters to develop a complete picture of what happens deep in the ground during an earthquake. When extreme pressure causes rocks inside the earth's surface to strain and break, an earthquake results. The pressure usually comes from the movement of the large plates that make up the earth's crust.

Most earthquakes begin at plate boundaries, which are the sites of the greatest strain and pressure. Earthquakes triggered by fault movement begin at a specific point along the fault, usually where the most pressure has resulted in the initial rupture. The energy released from the break originates at that point and spreads outward.

Identical Earthquakes, Centuries Apart

In 1999 a devastating earthquake shook Izmit, Turkey, killing thousands of people and leveling entire sections of the area, duplicating almost exactly the damage done by an earthquake that hit the same region in A.D. 358. A fascinating account by Ammianus Marcellinus, a fourth-century A.D. writer, reveals many similarities between the earthquake he experienced and the Izmit quake that struck in modern times. Marcellinus's description can be found on the U.S. Geological Survey website.

I shall give a true and concise account of the misfortune of [the earthquake's] destruction. On the twenty fourth of August, at the first break of the day, a terrific earthquake utterly destroyed the city and its suburbs. And since most of the houses were carried down the slopes of the hills, they fell one upon another, while everything resounded with the vast roar of their destruction. Meanwhile the hilltops re-echoed with all manner of outcries, of those seeking their wives, their children and their relatives. Finally, after the second hour, but well before the third, the air, which was now bright and clear, revealed the fatal ravages that lay concealed. For some who have been crushed by the huge bulk of the debris falling upon them perished under its very weight; some were buried up to their necks in the heaps of rubble, and might have survived had anyone helped them, but died for want of assistance; others hung impaled upon the sharp points of projecting timber. Most were killed instantly, and where there had been human beings shortly before, were now seen confused piles of corpses. Some were imprisoned unhurt within fallen house roofs, only to die in agony and starvation. . . . Others, who were overtaken by the suddenness of the disaster, still lay hidden under the ruins; some with fractured skulls or severed arms or legs hovered between life and death, imploring the aid of others in the same situation; but they were abandoned, despite their strong entreaties. And the greater part of the temples and private houses might have been saved, and of the population as well, had not a sudden onrush of flames, sweeping over them for five days and nights, burned up whatever could be consumed.

Scientists call the point where the rupture begins the focus of the earthquake. An earthquake's focus is almost always deep in the ground.

The point on the surface of the earth directly above the focus is the earthquake's epicenter. News agencies and the public usually think of the epicenter as the place where the greatest power and damage from an earthquake originates. This is not always true. In some cases, buildings and other structures near the epicenter of an earthquake suffer less damage than structures farther away. The epicenter is mainly a way for seismologists and geologists to pinpoint the location of an earthquake on a map. A map of earthquakes really shows a map of epicenters.

The initial fracture at the focus of the earthquake moves quickly along the fault surface, releasing all the pressure and energy that had been built up in the rocks. If the fracture is small, the earthquake will last only a few seconds. However, if the fracture is large, and if there has been a tremendous buildup of pressure, the earthquake can last much longer. A good example of this comes from the 1994 Northridge earthquake, noted by authors Kerry Sieh and Simon LeVay,

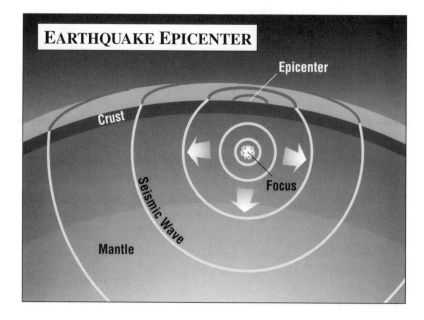

Eleven miles below the town of Northridge, in Los Angeles' San Fernando Valley, rock stressed to the breaking point had suddenly failed. A 10-mile side crack raced upward at 7,000 miles per hour, radiating enough energy to bring down freeways; knock houses off their foundations; and rupture gas, water, and power lines.[30]

During this fracturing process, a great deal of energy is released from the rocks around the fracture. Some of this energy radiates outward in all directions in the form of waves called seismic waves.

Seismic Waves

The motion that is felt during an earthquake is created by the seismic waves as they reach the earth's surface. Seismic waves cause the damage from an earthquake, and the rolling and heaving that people report during an earthquake are caused by the motion of seismic waves as they travel beneath the ground.

Some seismic waves move deep inside the earth; these are called body waves. Surface waves, as the name implies, are shallow, rolling ripples that travel just beneath the earth's surface. Some of the ground motion that does the most damage during an earthquake comes from surface waves. Surface waves are slower than body waves. Most earthquakes consist of both body waves and surface waves.

P Waves and S Waves

Scientists have classified body waves into two categories: primary and secondary waves. Primary waves are known as P waves, and secondary waves are called S waves.

P waves are the fastest seismic waves. The first jolt that a person feels during an earthquake is the arrival of the P waves. A P wave pushes and pulls rocks in a back-and-forth motion as it races through the ground. The action is similar to laying a Slinky on its side and tapping one end. The energy from the tap goes through the Slinky in a wave, pushing and pulling the coils back and forth. P waves can travel through solid rock, such as mountains, and also through water such as lakes and oceans.

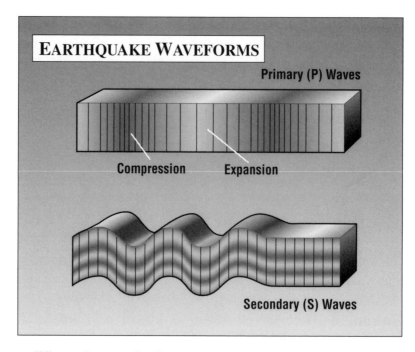

EARTHQUAKE WAVEFORMS

Primary (P) Waves

Compression   Expansion

Secondary (S) Waves

When a P wave finally reaches the earth's surface, the energy from the wave can sometimes become sound waves. The loud booms and cracks that are present during earthquakes are in fact P waves entering the atmosphere as sound waves.

It is the slower S waves, however, that produce the second series of motions that occur during an earthquake. As an S wave moves through the earth, it pushes the rock sideways in an undulating S-shaped motion. S waves travel in both up-and-down and side-to-side motions.

Seismic Waves Reflect and Refract

Although seismic waves travel in a straight line, they can also be reflected and refracted when they hit different kinds of rocks deep in the earth. These interruptions can cause seismic waves to change in intensity and power as they move through the earth. As a result, an earthquake consists of combinations of these waves hitting different areas at different times. Thus, people in one area of an earthquake might experience strong shaking and ground movement, while others only a short distance away may feel little or no earthquake movement. In some cases, people who have been in caves or mines deep in the earth during an earthquake have reported feeling little or no effects.

Unsurprisingly, then, most people feel a combination of forces during an earthquake. P waves usually strike first, followed by S waves, then some combination of reflected body waves and surface waves might come after that. One earthquake survivor's description highlights how the various waves felt as they hit:

> First there was a sudden jolt that made me lose my balance for a second. Then I could feel the ground moving, and a second, stronger jolt came. After a few seconds of shaking, a rolling and swaying motion started, like being on a boat. The swaying lasted until the earthquake ended. There was noise all the time.[31]

Measuring Earthquakes and Seismic Waves

The motion in the ground that is produced by earthquakes is recorded by instruments such as seismographs, or seismometers. Today, there are thousands of seismographs in locations throughout the world. They create a network used by geologists

Seismographs, like the one shown, record the motion in the ground when an earthquake strikes.

and seismologists to determine an earthquake's focus and epicenter. These seismographs can also measure how powerful the earthquake was and how long it lasted.

The initial seismic wave recorded at a seismograph station is the first evidence that an earthquake has occurred. Soon after, seismographs in other areas begin recording the waves as they hit. Geologists know approximately how fast seismic waves travel through different kinds of rocks, and they measure the arrival times of P waves and S waves at several different locations to plot the earthquake's epicenter and focus of the earthquake. Author Ellen J. Prager describes how scientists use the information from a number of seismograph stations to determine a focus:

> From one station, it is only possible to determine how far away the epicenter was from that individual station. The earthquake could have originated anywhere on a circle having a radius of that distance, with the station at its center. With two stations, two possible epicenters produce the right arrival time: where two circles, one drawn around each station, intersect. Data from a third station distinguishes between these two possible locations, and a fourth station adds enough information to determine the quake's depth within the Earth, its hypocenter [focus]. . . . Thus, having a network of seismic stations is essential for pinpointing the source of any earthquake. [32]

Once scientists determine the earthquake's focus and epicenter, they can alert the media and emergency management agencies where an earthquake has originated and approximately how severe the shocks were.

How a Seismograph Works

Seismographs measure ground movement during an earthquake. The earliest instruments consisted of a pendulum weight hung loosely from a frame that was attached to the earth, usually into bedrock. When the earth shook, the frame moved, indicating to observers that a seismic event was occurring. As Ellen J. Prager describes,

Seismographs

For centuries, people have tried to gauge the strength of earthquakes with mechanical devices. However, it was not until the late nineteenth century that a reliable device, called a seismograph, was developed.

John Milne, one of the earliest earthquake scientists, was a professor of geology and mining at the Imperial College of Engineering in Tokyo, Japan. He was interested in the earthquakes that rocked the country and attempted to monitor them. In the 1890s he created one of the first modern, accurate seismographs. Milne's seismograph was based on the principle of the pendulum. He suspended a weight from a frame and added a writing instrument—called a stylus—to the weight. Beneath the weight Milne placed a sheet of paper darkened by smoke and soot. When the earth trembled, the pendulum swung and the stylus recorded the movement with scratchy lines on the smoked paper. Later, Milne used photographic paper to trace the lines made by the earthquake.

Most modern seismographs use the same pendulum technology to record earthquakes. Seismographs now turn the earth's motion into electrical impulses that can be recorded on computers. Strong-motion seismographs are sturdy enough to record more powerful quakes. However, they all rely on the same basic idea that John Milne thought of more than one hundred years ago.

When the Earth moves either horizontally or vertically, the pendulum tends to stay still, at least momentarily, and then begins to move. The stronger the shaking, the larger the relative motion between the pendulum weight and the frame. . . . During an event [earthquake] the record of a pendulum's position over time looks like a zigzagging wave, slowly decreasing in size after the ground has stopped shaking.[33]

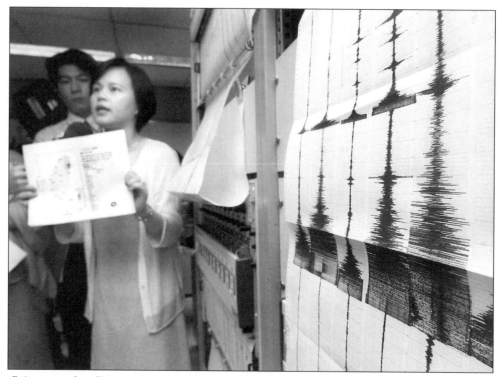

Seismographs allow scientists to measure the intensity and magnitude of an earthquake.

In the early days of seismology, the weight was fitted with some kind of recording implement, such as a pin, that scratched a line into black paper positioned beneath it. Modern seismographs still work like a pendulum, but they use a much more sophisticated mechanism that includes electromagnetic components. Inside the seismograph, the pendulum has a tightly wound coil of wire that hangs between two magnets. When seismic waves move the pendulum, an electric current is generated in the coil. The current can be used to move a writing instrument on paper, but it can also move a beam of light that records the quake on special photographic paper. The most sophisticated seismographs are attached to computers that record the data as it comes in.

Intensity and Magnitude

One of the first questions that the public asks when an earthquake strikes is "How big was it?" Once a seismograph has recorded an earthquake and scientists have pinpointed its location, they can determine how strong the earthquake was by measuring its intensity and magnitude. Intensity is the severity of the shaking that took place at a particular location. Magnitude is the size of the overall earthquake, as recorded by seismographs.

Centuries ago, people measured the strength of an earthquake in terms of the amount of damage it caused. If one earthquake caused more damage than another, people assumed that the second earthquake was stronger than the first. Eventually it became apparent that a single quake could cause many different kinds of damage, depending on a variety of conditions, including the location where the earthquake struck, the strength of the buildings, and the condition of the land.

Over the years, scientists have tried to develop a scale to measure an earthquake's power on the basis of the amount of damage it produced. One of the earliest attempts was made by Domenico Pignatoro, who set about classifying the hundreds of earthquakes that struck areas around Naples, Italy, from 1783 to 1786. He ranked quakes as slight, moderate, strong, and very strong. Science used this scale, or others like it, for decades.

Eventually, however, scientists realized that they needed a more precise way of measuring the damage intensity of earthquakes. In 1902 another Italian scientist, Giuseppe Mercalli, developed a more detailed scale. By the 1930s American seismologists modified Mercalli's scale to make it more useful. On the new scale, called the modified Mercalli scale, an earthquake with an intensity of I is not felt by humans. An earthquake with an intensity of XIII will completely destroy an area. The modified Mercalli scale is still used by many scientists today to rate the intensity of an earthquake.

Because the damage from a quake can vary greatly from place to place, one earthquake might have many intensities. For example, the intensity of the quake in farmland, where there are few buildings to be damaged, might be much lower than the intensity of the same quake in an urban area with many structures.

Although intensity scales are useful in pinpointing certain aspects of an earthquake, they are not very reliable in determining how powerful the earthquake was. To do that, scientists look at the magnitude of an earthquake, which is determined by the Richter scale. The scale, developed in 1935, was named for Charles Richter, a professor of seismology at the California Institute of Technology. Author D. S. Halacy Jr., tells why the professor was so honored:

> Dr. Richter saw the need to classify earthquakes by size just as astronomers classify stars according to their brightness (or magnitude). By setting up standards for seismographs and dis-

Dr. Richter, seen here standing beside a seismograph, developed the mathematical equation now used to identify the magnitude of an earthquake.

The Loma Prieta earthquake of 1989, which caused the San Francisco–Oakland Bay Bridge to collapse, measured 7.2 on the Richter scale.

tances from quakes, and working out methods for adjusting for differences in both seismograph and distances, Richter arrived at the quantity M, or Richter Magnitude. M is a measure of the amount of energy released by an earthquake.[34]

Richter used a complex system of mathematical equations to develop his M measurement. Once the calculations have been made, each earthquake is assigned a number from 1 to 10 based on its magnitude. On the Richter scale, each step up in magnitude means a tenfold increase in the power of the earthquake. For example, a 6.0 earthquake is ten times stronger than a 5.0 earthquake, a hundred times stronger than a 4.0 earthquake, and a thousand times stronger than a 3.0 earthquake.

So far, there has never been a magnitude 10 earthquake, which scientists believe would be a major catastrophic world event. Any earthquake over a magnitude 8 is considered to be extremely powerful, and earthquakes of that power are rarely recorded. Only four earthquakes in the twentieth century have ever measured a magnitude of 9 or above: the 1960 earthquake in Chile

(9.5); the 1964 Alaska earthquake (9.2); an earthquake in the Aleutian Islands near Alaska in 1957 (9.1); and the earthquake on Kamchatka, Russia in 1952 (9.0). As a comparison, the devastating Loma Prieta earthquake near San Francisco in 1989 measured 7.2 on the Richter scale.

In recent years, scientists have begun to question the precision of the Richter scale in determining the size of an earthquake. Many variables that can affect the power of the quake are not accounted for in the Richter scale. Today, many scientists and geologists use the power of seismic waves to calculate the strength of an earthquake, while others rely on complex mathematical equations that few people outside the scientific community can grasp. However, many others still use the Richter scale in a variety of ways.

Uses of Magnitude Measurements

Although many scientists now agree that the Richter scale is not the most precise way to measure earthquakes, scientists, the public, and engineers continue to use the Richter scale as a guide in determining the power of an earthquake. When an earthquake does strike, the Richter scale numbers are generally understood by most people. For example, most people realize that a 6.0 magnitude quake is far less powerful than a 7.0, and so on. The Richter scale is a simple way to relate information about the power of a quake to the general public.

Engineers and building designers also use the Richter scale model to develop earthquake-resistant structures. They research the magnitudes of previous quakes in an area, then they use those numbers to predict how powerful a future earthquake might be. Then the designers and engineers build a structure that will withstand the motions from a quake of that magnitude.

When an Earthquake Strikes

According to some earthquake studies, thousands of earthquakes shake the earth every day. The vast majority are hardly noticeable by people, and many occur far from populated areas. These quakes are recorded by delicate instruments at lonely seismographic monitoring stations. Yet according to authors Gere and Shah,

The likelihood that you will feel an earthquake is actually very high. It happens to most people several times during their lives. . . . On a worldwide basis, about one person in 8,000 will end his life in an earthquake, and ten times that many will be injured by an earthquake sometime during their lives.[35]

Many people who have survived an earthquake report similar experiences, beginning with loud and terrifying sounds. In some cases, the sounds of an earthquake can be heard before the shaking itself is felt. Author John Hodgson describes these sounds:

In accounts of earthquakes we always hear of the frightful noise which they produce, by the collapse of buildings or by their frantic motion, by the creaking of trees and the slapping together of their branches . . . by the rushing of air and water . . . by the crash of landslides.[36]

A few seconds of strong shaking in an earthquake can cause extensive damage.

The sounds of an earthquake are usually immediately followed by a large jolt. After a few seconds, another jolt hits and the shaking begins. Soon the shaking starts to inflict damage, as Gere and Shah describe:

> Window glass cracks and breaks, objects fall off the shelves, bookcases topple, light fixtures fall from the ceilings, and cracks appear in the walls, floors, and ceilings. The noise is deafening. It takes only a dozen seconds of strong shaking to wreck an entire building, sometimes even bringing it to the ground. The longer the shaking continues, the more severe the damage. [37]

People report that the earth outside moves like waves on an ocean. Trees sway and topple, as do power lines and other structures. Roads and sidewalks crack and break apart. In some cases, sections of land drop or rise with thunderous noise. When it is over, everything is in shambles. The earthquake lasted only a few seconds, but the destruction may well be complete.

After the Shock

O n a cold December morning in 1988, a series of devastating earthquakes shook Armenia. This area of the world has been plagued by earthquakes for centuries, and severe tremors have been recorded there as far back as 550 B.C. But as with most earthquakes, this one came as a terrible shock to the citizens of Armenia, as one author explained:

The first of these devastating earthquakes radiated out from a rupturing fault at 11:41 A.M. local time and affected a

A devastating earthquake shook Armenia in 1988, killing up to twenty-five thousand people and destroying countless homes and businesses.

population of 700,000 people, destroying large sections of the cities of Spitak, Leninakan and Kirovakan. In the surrounding countryside, 58 villages were leveled and 100 significantly damaged. One government estimate was that 25,000 people perished, based on the recovery of 24,944 bodies from the rubble. The earthquake left at least 514,000 homeless and 30,000 injured. . . . Parts of the area of strongest ground [were] highly industrialized with both light and heavy industry, such as large chemical and food processing plants. There [were] a number of large electrical substations, thermal power plants, in this area; many were affected.[38]

Later the official death toll would rise to more than fifty-five thousand, with hundreds of thousands more injured and homeless. The destruction in the area was almost total. Survivors wandered among the rubble, dazed. In some places, no buildings were left standing. In the large towns and the small villages, people were stunned at the amount of damage this earthquake produced. Although the earthquake was a powerful 7.0, it caused more damage than scientists might have thought. One report summarized the extensive destruction of this earthquake:

The catastrophic earthquake that occurred on December 7, 1988, brought about heavy damage to most buildings and structures in many cities and villages. Initial results of our investigation revealed that in its manifestation most frame and nine-story frame panel buildings were completely destroyed. Stone buildings with no anti-seismic measures of construction collapsed. In large areas, there was large deformation of railroads and distortion of railtracks. Rock slides occurred in the mountains. Wide cracks appeared in the soil; there were massive slides along cliffs. Bridges were greatly damaged. In the city of Leninakan industrialized enterprises and trade centers collapsed and the chemical plant in the city of Kirovakan was wrecked. In Spitak, commercial enterprises were completely destroyed; educational institutions such as schools, nurseries, maternity wards and hospitals were lost in most cases.[39]

In spite of strict building codes, the 1995 earthquake that struck Kobe, Japan, destroyed large sections of the city.

No one could explain the extent of the destruction in Armenia, so scientists put forth many theories. Some suggested that the earthquake was simply more powerful than originally thought. Others believed that the damage was more extensive because many of the cities were near major fault lines. Ultimately, however, it was determined that the main reason for the destruction was that the buildings had not been constructed to withstand such a powerful earthquake. That fact, combined with other destructive forces of an earthquake, resulted in the almost total destruction of the cities in Armenia.

Since 1988 devastating earthquakes have occurred in other areas of the world. In 1995, Kobe, Japan, was rocked by an earthquake that destroyed large sections of the city. The widespread damage in Kobe was even more disturbing to world scientists because Japan has some of the most advanced earthquake resistant building codes in the world. No one expected the destruction in Kobe to be as massive as it was—collapsed buildings, destroyed bridges and railway systems, and widespread breakdown of vital services such as the water supply were common.

Safety Rules During an Earthquake

Experiencing an earthquake can be terrifying. Following certain safety rules during an earthquake can make the experience less frightening. The American Red Cross website lists the following safety rules.

1. When in a high-rise building, move against an interior wall if you are not near a desk or table. Protect your head with your arms. Do not use elevators.

2. When outdoors, move to a clear area away from trees, signs, buildings, or downed electrical wires and poles.

3. When on a sidewalk near buildings, duck into a doorway to protect yourself from falling bricks, glass, plaster, or other debris.

4. When driving, pull over to the side of the road and stop. Avoid overpasses and power lines. Stay inside your vehicle until the shaking stops.

5. When in a crowded store or other public place, move away from display shelves containing objects that could fall. Do not rush for the exit.

6. When in a stadium or theater, stay in your seat, get below the level of the back of the seat and cover your head with your arms.

Above all, remain calm. Most injuries occur because people panick and do not remember safety rules.

A few years later thousands died when another earthquake destroyed the area of Izmit, Turkey. As in Armenia and Kobe, the destruction in Turkey in 1999 surprised and sobered many scientists. More recently, earthquakes in Papua New Guinea on November 16, 2000, and in El Salvador, Central America, on January 13, 2001, claimed thousands of lives and affected countless people.

Thus the brief, terrible period in which the ground shakes, rolls, and bucks is far from the only dangerous aspect of an earthquake. The most destructive forces of an earthquake come after the shock.

Earthquake Hazards

During an earthquake, the actual shaking of the earth poses little danger to people. No one can be shaken to death by an earthquake. Nor do huge cracks open up in the earth and appear to swallow people, as is sometimes portrayed in movies. The shaking does create other, very dangerous hazards. Seismologists classify earthquake hazards as either natural or man-made. Natural hazards are those that occur in nature, such as landslides, ground liquefaction [the process of becoming liquid], ground displacement, and tsunamis. Man-made hazards are such disasters as floods from broken dams or fires, caused largely by ruptured gas lines.

A fireman directs water onto a fire caused by an earthquake. Fires often occur after earthquakes due to ruptured gas lines.

Landslides

Landslides occur during an earthquake when the shaking of the ground loosens soil, rocks, and sometimes ice from mountain-tops. This debris crashes down the mountain face, destroying everything in its path. One of the most devastating earthquake landslides occurred on May 31, 1970, in Peru. The epicenter of that earthquake was off the coast of Peru near the city of Chimbote, but the shaking loosened debris at the top of Mount Huascarán, eighty miles from the earthquake. Authors Gere and Shah describe the devastation that followed:

> Gathering speed and mass as it rushed down the mountain, the slide quickly assumed tremendous proportions. It sped at over 200 kilometers per hour (120 mph) down a long val-ley, filling it with rock, ice, and mud, and partially destroy-ing the town of Ranrahirca, located about 12 kilometers below the mountain. Part of the landslide branched off to one side, swept over a high ridge, and roared through the village of Yungay. The village was obliterated; only a few of its inhabitants were able to escape by running to higher ground as the landslide approached. One survivor likened the oncoming slide to a gigantic breaker coming in from the ocean with a deafening roar and rumble—it was, in fact over 30 meters (100 feet) high.[40]

More than eighteen thousand people were buried by the land-slide, and the total number of people killed by the slide is estimated at twenty-five thousand. The earthquake caused many other, smaller landslides in the region, destroying thousands of buildings in other villages. When this earthquake was over, more than sixty-seven thousand people had died, most of them from landslides.

One of the most recent earthquakes, which hit the Central American country of El Salvador in January 2001, was accompa-nied by devastating landslides on the slopes of a nearby volcano. One U.S. Geological Survey report described the destruction:

> Preliminary reports from El Salvador state that there is addi-tional, widespread landsliding due to the latest El Salvador earthquake. This [the latest in a series of] quake[s] occurred

Following an earthquake in January 2001, a landslide buried five hundred homes in one neighborhood of San Salvador, capital city of El Salvador.

on Tuesday, February 13. . . . Many landslides have blocked roads, impeding rescue efforts for victims of the quake and landslides. Rescuers are trying to reach the slopes of Chichontepec Volcano, where [many] people are said to have been buried by landslides. This mountain is near San Vicente, a city hit hard by the quake, about 30 miles east of the capital, San Salvador. Helicopter overflights by the press report widespread landslides on the slopes of the volcano.[41]

Alaska is also an area of seismic activity, and huge landslides have accompanied earthquakes there. One of the largest occurred on July 9, 1958. An earthquake set off a landslide on the side of a mountain near Lituya Bay. The landslide moved quickly, according to authors Gere and Shah:

A huge mass of rock and soil rushed downward, denuding the mountainside and exposing the base rock beneath. The moving mass crashed into the northern arm of the bay, rushed across it, and still had enough momentum to carry the slide material up the mountain on the opposite side, scraping the mountain clean of its forest cover to a height of over 300 meters (900 feet).[42]

A smaller earthquake-induced landslide occurred on August 17, 1959. That day, an earthquake started a landslide on a mountain above the Madison River in Montana, west of Yellowstone National Park. According to some reports, the landslide contained more than 80 million tons of rock and debris:

> The slide came down the side of the mountain and swept over a campground, burying forever a number of campers with their tents and vehicles. Then it rushed into the river, completely filling it, and continued up the mountain slope on the far side. The flow of the river was stopped by this natural dam until the new lake was filled.[43]

The lake, now called Earthquake Lake, still exists. Visitors can see where the landslide crashed down the mountain and marvel at the power that created a new lake.

Liquefaction

One of the most common and dangerous hazards of an earthquake is liquefaction, a phenomenon that occurs when the earthquake's vibration causes soil to change from a firm material to a semiliquid material, similar to quicksand. Liquefaction can devastate large areas or it can create small pockets of semiliquid soil, which scientists refer to as boils. Liquefaction is most common in areas where the soil contains sand and water, such as in low-lying areas near the sea, marshlands, rivers, or lakes.

One area that is prone to liquefaction is the coastal area of Washington State. In February 2001, a 6.8 magnitude earthquake struck Harbor Island, south of downtown Seattle. U.S. Geological Survey seismologist Bob Norris witnessed firsthand the liquefaction process:

> I was distracted by a wet swishing sound coming from the ground nearby. I . . . saw a smooth dome of brown fluid, perhaps a foot and a half wide and high, issuing from the ground

a few yards away. . . . This dome lasted perhaps two seconds, then grew and burst into a muddy geyser. This geyser issued three or four very fluid splashes over the next few seconds, about a yard high each, then it widened and collapsed into a column about half that wide that discharged a tremendous volume of muddy water. . . . Within a few seconds the flow front had become a surge several inches high, like a small wave traveling up a dry beach. . . . Within 30 seconds, the surge had grown into a shallow rotating pool about 25 feet across with bits of suds floating on it, still vigorously fed by the column of water at the original breakout site.[44]

When liquefaction occurs during an earthquake, structures built on the soft soil may not be damaged, but the liquefaction causes them to tilt, collapse, or settle into the ground. One example occurred in Japan in 1964, as described by author Bolt:

The streets of Seatle, Washington, are littered with debris after a 6.8 magnitude earthquake hit in February 2001.

Liquefaction of sandy foundations, in many cases, has disastrous effects on structures. In the earthquake that much affected Niigata in Japan in 1964, reinforced concrete buildings, otherwise structurally undamaged, tilted calamitously because of the liquefaction of the underlying soil. Failures of walls along harbor facilities and bridge piers and embankments were also quite severe. [45]

As a result of the 1989 Loma Prieta earthquake, a large section of Interstate 880 collapsed in Oakland, California.

Protecting Against Liquefaction

Over the years, scientists and engineers have tried to lessen the effects of liquefaction by a variety of methods. One such method, vibroflotation, compacts soft soil so that it is less likely to liquefy. Large machinery creates vibrations in the ground and pumps water in at the same time. The combination of the vibrations and the added pressure of the water causes the soil to liquefy, then to compact.

Another solution is to dig underground drains and remove the underlying water, thereby lessening the chance of liquefaction. A third method is to excavate the layer of soil that might liquefy. However, all of these methods are expensive, and most home builders do not use them. Most people who knowingly build on soft soil simply hope that an earthquake will not strike.

Ground Displacement

An earthquake hazard even more serious than liquefaction is ground displacement, or ground subsidence. During an earthquake, the shaking causes the soil to compact and create depressions in the landscape. The effect is similar to shaking a box of cereal to settle it. When there is little water however, the ground does not liquefy into a quicksand-like material.

The type of soil that is most likely to be displaced is loose soil such as landfill. This type of soil tends to shake more during an earthquake, causing greater damage. One of the most striking examples of ground deformation during an earthquake was seen in the 1989 Loma Prieta earthquake in California. Most of the damage and deaths were caused by ground deformation, as authors Sieh and LeVay comment:

> Perhaps the most fateful reason for local differences in shaking severity is the nature of the soil. Other things being equal, loose, uncompacted soil or landfill will always shake more than solid rock. . . . [This] happened in the Loma Prieta earthquake; many houses subsided or collapsed in the Marina district, which is built on landfill. The portion of Interstate 880 that collapsed in Oakland, killing many motorists, was also constructed on landfill.[46]

Another tragic example of the danger of ground deformation occurred in the 1985 Mexico City earthquake. Although the focus of the quake was more than two hundred miles away, the tremors created massive ground deformation in parts of the city that were built on soft lakebed sediments. The resulting building collapses killed more than eight thousand people.

Fires

Raging fires are of serious concern after an earthquake. During an earthquake, ruptured gas lines or toppled electrical lines can pose a fire threat. During the 1906 San Francisco earthquake, most buildings survived the shaking but were destroyed by the fires that consumed the city soon after. As author Bolt relates:

> Soon after the San Francisco earthquake, fires broke out in several places and spread for three days, burning 508 blocks of the city. The main problems were the highly combustible nature of many buildings, the lack of fire protective devices such as sprinklers, and the narrow streets. The ground shaking caused the city water-pipe system to break in hundreds of places so that, although there was ample water in the distribution reservoirs, little was available in the burning areas. [47]

After the 1971 San Fernando earthquake, 109 fires broke out in the city, mainly caused by broken gas lines. During the 1994 Northridge earthquake, many fires were also ignited by broken gas lines. Authors Sieh and LeVay were eyewitnesses to the destruction caused by that quake, including fires that raged in parts of the San Fernando Valley. They described one fire they saw:

> Destruction was everywhere. Buildings had collapsed, trains had derailed, fires were burning, and burst mains were spraying fountains of water skyward. At one location . . . several fire-gutted homes surrounded a roiling fireball in the middle of the street. The fire was being fed by a broken gas main. . . . The escaping gas had been ignited by a motorist attempting to restart his engine, which had stalled. . . . The truck was thrown into the air and charred by the explosion, but neither the man

These houses were destroyed by fire after the 1994 Northridge, California, earthquake.

nor his dog were hurt. It was more than a year later that USGS [U.S. Geological Survey] geologists determined that the gas and water main ruptures had been caused by liquefaction-induced ground cracking.[48]

Floods

One of the most terrifying possibilities of disaster during an earthquake is a dam failure. Millions of people live in the areas below major dams, and most are not aware that they could be in danger from a massive flood if the dam crumbled during a tremor.

Two devastating dam failures during past earthquakes highlight this danger. In 1925 a large earthquake rocked the California city of Santa Barbara, and the nearby Sheffield Dam collapsed. It released more than 40 million gallons of water, flooding large sections of the city and killing many. During the 1971 San Fernando earthquake in California, the Van Norman Dam was damaged so

Workmen assess the damage to the Van Norman Dam caused by the 1971 San Fernando earthquake.

badly that it could not be repaired. Tens of thousands of people had to be evacuated from below the dam. In both cases, the dams were earthen dams, and the failure was caused by liquefaction.

In most earthquake-prone areas, modern building codes forbid the construction of dams from earth or fill. Dams built according to these codes should be able to withstand a mild to medium earthquake with no significant damage.

Tsunamis

Flooding also occurs as part of another earthquake hazard, tsunamis. *Tsunami* is a Japanese word meaning bay or tidal wave. It is used throughout the world to describe the enormous ocean waves that pound coastal areas after an earthquake.

In most cases, tsunamis are generated from earthquakes that occur deep in the ocean floor. These quakes usually originate at subduction zones where two tectonic plates meet. Authors Gere and Shah describe how a deep-ocean earthquake creates a tsunami:

> As the stresses build up . . . relief occurs in the form of sudden slippage, which, of course, is an earthquake. Since the slippage involves upward movement of the sea bottom, it also causes an upward movement of the overlying sea water.

When a large volume of sea water is suddenly uplifted, huge surface waves are created that spread outward in all directions. When these waves rush onto land at a nearby coast . . . they are called local tsunamis. These local waves have caused great loss of life on the coasts of Japan, the Philippines, South America, and the eastern Mediterranean Sea.[49]

The waves of a tsunami are not like ordinary ocean waves. The energy from the earthquake causes a series of underwater waves that can move quickly across great distances in the ocean. These waves move like sound waves through the water, and they stretch from the surface of the ocean all the way to the bottom. Because the waves radiate in all directions, one earthquake can create tsunamis that affect coastlines in many different areas.

As a tsunami gets closer to a coast, the enormous energy it contains becomes compressed in a smaller area as the ocean becomes shallower. That is when the tsunami creates the enormous walls of water that strike a beach or coastline.

The biggest terror of tsunamis is that they hit without much warning. Many witnesses have described calm, ordinary ocean and beach conditions minutes before a tsunami arrived. Others have recounted a strange phenomenon in which the water of the ocean appears to recede, or empty. People wander onto the wet sand, marveling at the flopping fish and other stranded sea life, only to be consumed by the gigantic wave that sweeps upon them.

One of the most horrific tsunamis in history struck the coast of Papua, New Guinea, on Friday, July 17, 1998. One magazine article described the terrible events of that evening:

Shortly before sunset, the earth began to shake, and a thunderous boom shattered the air. Large cracks

On July 17, 1998, Papua, New Guinea, was hit by one of the most horrific tsunamis in history.

suddenly gaped open on the beach, and the village children, filled with curiosity, ran to look, encouraging the grown-ups to come and see, too. As a crowd gathered, the ocean began to recede from the shore, and, as the water drew farther out, a distant murmur grew to a rumbling. Within a few minutes the rumbling had grown to a deafening roar, like the sound of an approaching jet squadron. The sea had returned as a wall of water, glowing red near the crest. As the watchers turned to flee, the wave broke offshore, surging through the villages and knocking people off their feet. . . . On the heels of the first, a second monstrous wave swept in. This one crashed directly over [the villages of] Warapu and Arop, engulfing the villagers as they raced inland, and drove landward for hundreds of meters. The dead and brutally injured were dumped into the lagoon and surrounding mangroves. When the wave retreated, it pulled many of the victims out to sea. [50]

On average, one tsunami occurs somewhere in the world every year. A tsunami can be created by earthquakes in any ocean or sea, but they seem to be most common in the Pacific, Indian, Mediterranean, Atlantic, and Caribbean.

Relief and Rescue Efforts

When an earthquake strikes, it is imperative that relief and rescue efforts begin immediately. National agencies and organizations, as well as local government agencies, are usually the first to an earthquake disaster site. Most state divisions of the U.S. National Guard, for instance, are well trained to respond to such disasters. They provide humanitarian assistance such as food, water, medical attention, and shelter to the hundreds, or thousands, of victims of an earthquake. The Red Cross also provides food, shelter, and medical help.

But meeting basic human needs is only a part of what must be done in the aftermath of a quake. In many cases, victims are trapped beneath tons of rubble. They must be located and rescued as quickly as possible, so some groups use specially trained dogs to locate people still alive beneath the debris. Roads must be cleared for emergency transports to hospitals and for trucks car-

Cities at Greatest Risk for Earthquakes

The Federal Emergency Management Agency (FEMA) has developed a list of the major U.S. cities that face the greatest earthquake danger and losses from an earthquake. The top ten cities in the U.S. at the greatest risk:

1. Los Angeles, California
2. Riverside, California
3. Oakland, California
4. San Francisco, California
5. San Jose, California
6. Orange, California
7. Seattle, Washington
8. San Diego, California
9. Portland, Oregon
10. Ventura, California

Other major U.S. cities on the list include New York City (11); Salt Lake City, Utah (14); St. Louis, Missouri (16); Las Vegas, Nevada (22); Memphis, Tennessee (27); Charleston, South Carolina (31); and Newark, New Jersey (33).

rying medical supplies, food, water, and other essentials to the disaster site. Basic human needs, such as areas to bathe and places to dispose of waste must be set up and maintained. In an area that has been demolished by an earthquake, meeting these simple needs becomes an enormous problem.

Furthermore, repair crews must reestablish communication and transportation lines, sewer and plumbing systems, and other necessary city services so that victims can be cared for. If many people are left homeless, arrangements for suitable housing must be made, places where they will live until their homes can be rebuilt or until they can relocate elsewhere. And relief groups must coordinate getting clothing and other personal items to the people who have been left with nothing.

Fires too, are always a threat throughout the affected area, so firefighters and rescue teams are kept busy controlling fires and assisting survivors. These professionals, along with local police, sometimes also have the job of evacuating people whose homes are unsafe. Fortunately, most cities in earthquake-prone zones have emergency plans already in place in case of a devastating

After an earthquake, rescue teams must search through masses of rubble for survivors.

earthquake. However, the task of aiding the victims is enormous and can take thousands of people and millions of dollars to complete.

Science Springs into Action

The 1994 Northridge, California, earthquake left more than forty thousand people homeless and as many as sixteen thousand homes unsafe. Immediately following the earthquake, city emergency services such as police, fire departments, medical emergency teams, and even ordinary citizens worked around the clock to rescue people and fight fires. In the meantime, city managers were faced not only with the destruction in the city but with helping the thousands of residents who were displaced by the quake. Scientists and engineers from the U.S. Geological Survey (USGS) joined together to help the emergency managers cope with the disaster. Scientists prepared a shaking-intensity map for all of the greater Los Angeles area that showed the places where the severest shaking probably occurred and where the most extensive damage might be. This map helped city leaders to pinpoint where help was needed most and to send emergency teams to those areas. It also helped relief workers to know where the most victims might be so they could focus their energy in the hardest-hit areas.

The shaking-intensity map prepared by the scientists was the first one to be used after an earthquake. Both scientists and city planners realized what a vital tool it would be for future earthquakes.

Can We Predict
Earthquakes?

China is one of the most earthquake-prone countries in the world. For centuries the Chinese have tried to predict earthquakes, but with no success. Then, in 1974, the only accurately predicted earthquake in modern times took place there.

The region near the city of Haicheng in Liaoning Province had been monitored for several years. Seismologists had installed many instruments in the area to record earthquake predictors such as tilting of land surfaces, changes in the electrical activity in the ground, and fluctuations in the magnetic field. Area residents helped the scientists by reporting odd animal behavior or a drop in the well water levels—two things that many believe are precursors to an earthquake.

By January 1975 seismologists agreed, based on the evidence, that there would likely be an earthquake in the near future. Authorities put the city on alert and began preparations for evacuating the population. Scientists continued to monitor the area, and by the evening of February 3 they agreed that an earthquake was imminent. The next morning, a small 4.7 magnitude earthquake hit the area.

Local officials sprang into action. Police and fire companies were warned, disaster relief agencies were alerted, and people were encouraged to leave their homes and camp out-of-doors. At 7:36 P.M. on February 4, a magnitude 7.3 earthquake rocked the city. Many parts of Haicheng were damaged or destroyed. Remarkably, there were few deaths because most people had heeded the warning and remained outside, even though it had

Despite great damage to buildings, few people were hurt during an earthquake in China in 1974 because seismologists were able to predict its occurrance and warn the population.

been bitterly cold. Scientists around the world were shocked to hear the news of the successful earthquake prediction, and for years afterward hope was high that the feat could be repeated elsewhere.

Unfortunately, that hope was premature. Since the Haicheng earthquake prediction, geologists have tried to successfully predict when and where an earthquake will strike. But the answers continue to elude science. Today, most scientists have focused their efforts in studying changes in the seismological features of the land; these changes might indicate that a large earthquake is about to occur. If they can pinpoint specific precursors to a large earthquake, it might be more likely to predict the next high-intensity, high-magnitude quake.

Many scientists think that someday a way will be found to predict a large quake. They point to the Haicheng prediction as evidence that earthquakes can be forecast. Others believe that earthquake prediction is impossible. According to these skeptics, every area of the world has its own unique characteristics and dangers, meaning that a uniform method of prediction cannot be made. Even the great Charles Richter, for whom the Richter magnitude scale is named, did not believe that anyone could ever predict earthquakes. He once wrote:

> Don't worry about predictions. The danger is real, and you may find yourself involved in a destructive earthquake five minutes from now; but no one can tell you when. Claims to predict usually come from cranks, publicity seekers, or people who pretend to foresee the future in general. Scientific men speaking about the general earthquake danger, and mentioning the likelihood of strong earthquakes in the near

The Parkfield Earthquake Prediction Experiment

For years scientists have attempted to predict earthquakes by researching the history of earthquake-prone areas. One such area is in central California along the San Andreas Fault. In this area, the fault stretches through open, remote land near a town called Parkfield. Seismographs at the University of California have recorded regular earthquake activity in the area since 1901, suggesting that quakes hit the area about every twenty-two years. Based on that data, scientists decided to attempt to predict the next earthquake that would hit Parkfield.

The U.S. Geological Survey dubbed the project the Parkfield Earthquake Prediction Experiment. As a result of the historical cycle of earthquakes, seismologists predicted that the next large quake would hit before 1993. Many speculated that 1988 would be the year of the big quake. During that year, scientists watched the area carefully, but no earthquake occurred.

The year 1993 also came and went without a major earthquake, although a number of smaller quakes did shake the area during that time. Finally, scientists conceded that their prediction experiment had failed.

Then they began to question why the prediction failed. Some scientists speculate that other, larger earthquakes in California had disrupted the pattern at Parkfield, overruling the prediction that a quake would hit by 1993. Others suggested that the earthquake clues at Parkfield were simply not reliable enough to accurately predict a large earthquake.

Today, seismologists continue to measure the earthquake activity at Parkfield. They hope that what they learned by the failed prediction there will enable them to successfully predict earthquakes elsewhere in the future.

future are often misrepresented as making definite predictions. If, after a strong earthquake, you hear or read that "another big one is expected," do not be unduly alarmed. It is probably a mistake (to put the matter mildly.) [51]

Early Attempts at Prediction

Since ancient times people have tried to predict earthquakes. Some believed that earthquakes could be predicted by watching the movements of the stars and planets in the sky. The ancient Greek scholar Anaximander once warned of an earthquake based on his study of the heavens, although there is no record to suggest that an earthquake actually occurred.

For centuries, people have claimed to see unusual animal behavior before an earthquake. In Japan, people believed that catfish became sensitive and restless before an earthquake. Interestingly, Japanese legends about earthquakes include a giant catfish. Citizens of Haicheng reported bizarre animal behavior before the 1974 earthquake, including snakes that came out of hibernation too early and froze to death. It is possible that animals sense a change in the earth prior to an earthquake, such as a fluctuation in the electric or magnetic fields. However, it is difficult to know if the odd behavior was caused by the quake or something else.

Today, most geologists dismiss the ancient prediction beliefs, focusing instead on studying measurable scientific clues. They hope that these clues will one day be used to successfully predict earthquakes. So far most scientific methods have met with little success, but all acknowledge the usefulness of recognizing any clues in the land or in nature that might warn of an impending quake. Aside from hints provided by observed changes, however, one tool many would-be earthquake prognosticators use is the familiar weathercaster's standby: probability.

Probability

If an earthquake has struck in a certain place, at a certain time, with a certain magnitude, it is probable that a similar earthquake will occur at that same place sometime in the future. As one scientist explains:

Attempting to predict an earthquake, scientists examine a fault line.

Scientists study the past frequency of large earthquakes in order to determine the future likelihood of similar large shocks. For example, if a region has experienced four magnitude 7 or larger earthquakes during 200 years of recorded history, and if these shocks occurred randomly in time, then scientists would assign a 50 percent probability (that just as likely to happen as not to happen) to the occurrence of another magnitude 7 or larger quake in the region during the next 50 years.[52]

Many scientists are skeptical of the value of applying this method to earthquakes, however. They argue when strain is released from one area of a fault, it may actually increase the strain in another area rather than allowing the strain to subside. Or if an earthquake released strain in a number of areas, this could mean that the region would not have another serious earthquake for a very long time afterward.

Rock Strain

Another way that scientists and geologists try to predict earth-quakes is to study the strain in the rocks of a fault. When plates move, they build strain in the rocks to a very high level. At some point the strain will be too much and the rocks will break, slip-ping into a new position as the strain is released. Scientists mon-itor how much strain accumulates in various areas of a section of a fault each year, how much time has passed since the last earth-quake in that fault segment, and how much strain was released in the last quake. They use this information to calculate how long it might take for the strain to build up to a point where it would be released, causing an earthquake.

Although this method sounds very simple, it is in fact compli-cated, largely because of the difficulty of obtaining detailed in-formation on the amount of strain in the world's faults. They are in inaccessible places, like at the bottom of oceans or deep un-derground. In the United States, the only fault system scientists can study closely is the San Andreas Fault. In any event, scien-tists have discovered that an increase in strain does not indicate whether an earthquake will happen at all, and if it does, how strong it might be.

Tilting Ground and Swarming Quakes

Scientists have noted that in many cases, the ground near the epi-center of an earthquake tilted or moved in the weeks and months before the quake struck. They believe that monitoring the ground tilt of an area prone to earthquakes might be a way to predict the next large event. Scientists monitoring the area around Haicheng observed and documented ground tilt, which helped them to pre-dict the earthquake that shook the area.

To measure ground tilt, scientists install sensitive instruments called tiltmeters in a number of places around the fault, and sci-entists carefully monitor the data they record about ground move-ments. Tiltmeters are so precise, say authors Gere and Shah, that "an instrument in California could measure the tilt of the United States if New York were lifted a mere 5 centimeters (or 2 inches)."[53]

Tiltmeter precision notwithstanding, however, ground tilt does not always herald the arrival of a major earthquake. In some cases, earthquakes occur with no ground movement, and in other cases a significant change in ground tilt is followed by minor tremors. For example, along the San Andreas fault, tiltmeters have recorded significant changes in ground tilt right before very small earthquakes.

Another seismological phenomenon that sometimes heralds a major tremor is an earthquake swarm. Many scientists have noted that sometimes large earthquakes are preceded by a great number of smaller shocks, usually very close together. The occurrence of such swarms before the Haicheng earthquake helped to convince scientists that a large earthquake was about to strike. Since then, scientists have studied earthquake swarms to determine whether they would be an accurate earthquake predictor. The swarms occur quite frequently, however, and a large earthquake rarely follows them.

The San Andreas Fault is the only fault system in the United States that scientists can study closely.

Release of Gases

Scientists around the world have noted that gases such as radon are released into the atmosphere prior to large earthquakes. This gas release usually occurs along active fault zones. Faults normally release these gases during quiet times, and in some cases very high concentrations of the gases seep from weaker sections of a fault. Scientists speculate that a great fluctuation in the release of these gases might be a clue that an earthquake is imminent.

But as with other clues to earthquake prediction, this one is also flawed, as author Bolt explains:

The same levels of [gas] fluctuation, however, have been found both before and after earthquakes and in many studies without any earthquake occurring at all. Because the geological environment varies so much, it has been impossible to determine whether earthquake-associated increases are exceptions to the normal variations in gas concentration.[54]

Electrical Activity

Electricity can be conducted through the ground, and some scientists believe that monitoring the electric current through certain types of rocks might predict earthquakes. Indeed, rocks such as granite, which have a high water content, are known to respond to extremely high pressures by showing major changes in their electrical resistance. Laboratory investigators have conducted experiments to test the electrical activity in rocks subjected to pressure, similar to the pressure that might occur immediately before an

In an attempt to predict earthquakes, scientists study changes in electrical conductivity that rocks display when subjected to pressure.

A timely earthquake prediction could allow city officials and emergency crews time to prepare.

earthquake. The granite specimens showed significant changes in their electrical resistance just before they fractured.

On the basis of this finding, scientists suggest that if certain rocks are monitored, the changes in their electrical content would indicate an earthquake. However, the few experiments to test this theory have been inconclusive.

The Problems with Predicting an Earthquake

Even if scientists were to predict an earthquake, no one is clear about how that prediction would be made public or what impact it might have on the population. On one hand, a timely prediction would enable city officials to create and execute evacuation plans, establish emergency sites, and mobilize resources such as police and fire departments. People would have time to prepare for the quake, and thousands of lives could be saved.

On the other hand, the alarming news of an impending earthquake might well cause a panic, with highways jammed with fleeing residents. Abandoned homes and other buildings would be vulnerable to theft and looting, which would put additional strains on local law-enforcement agencies. City resources would be stretched thin trying to control the situation. In more extreme cases, an earthquake prediction—especially one in which the predicted quake would not occur for days or weeks—could cause businesses to shut down and companies to close. This scenario has the potential to seriously affect the economy of an area.

Ultimately, most scientists agree that a reliable means of earthquake prediction does not yet exist and is unlikely to appear soon. Ellen J. Prager summarizes this view:

> The bottom line on earthquake prediction is a simple message: don't count on it happening. Research on earthquake prediction is still being conducted at several institutions, but the prospects are not as promising as they seemed after the Haicheng success. Reliable earthquake prediction is clearly complex and remains a thing of the future.[55]

Scientist Ruth Ludwin concurs in this, saying:

> It may never be possible to predict the exact time when a damaging earthquake will occur, because when enough strain has built up, a fault may become inherently unstable, and any small background earthquake may or may not continue rupturing and turn into a large earthquake. While it may eventually be possible to accurately diagnose the strain state of faults, the precise timing of large events may continue to elude us.[56]

Reducing Earthquake Risks

Although science cannot yet reliably predict earthquakes, a variety of studies through the years have revealed a great deal of information about how the earth and structures behave during a quake. Armed with this information, scientists hope to save lives and property when an earthquake strikes.

One of the first steps in reducing earthquake risks is to determine where earthquakes are most likely to hit, and where they are likely to do the most damage. Scientists, city officials, builders, and other personnel are beginning to work together in earthquake-prone areas such as California to develop seismic hazard maps. As Ellen J. Prager explains, "Seismic hazard mapping begins by studying a region's geology and locating all the faults within the area that could produce earthquakes. A wide array of techniques are used to locate, map, and study fault patterns."[57]

Seismic maps can be beneficial to scientists and city planners in a variety of ways. They can help engineers design bridges and highway structures that will stand up to an earthquake in certain

Seismic hazard mapping locates all the faults that can produce earthquakes in an area.

areas. Building codes that include earthquake-resistant rules for structures can be created. Scientists can assess the possibilities of earthquake-related disasters such as landslides, liquefaction, and other hazards.

Building Codes

The biggest challenge for city planners and engineers is to design structures that will withstand an earthquake. Most of the deaths

When a large earthquake struck Gujarat, India, on January 26, 2001, many structures collapsed.

Building Stronger Structures

Injury and death from building collapse is the greatest threat during an earthquake. Most people can survive, however, as long as the structures they are in can withstand the shaking earth.

Over the years, as devastating earthquakes have struck throughout the world, scientists have realized that some structures are much safer than others. For example, the masonry and concrete buildings in Armenia, Turkey, and Central America are not reinforced with steel rods, which stabilize the concrete. As a result, these structures cannot withstand even moderate shaking and will usually collapse, causing serious loss of life. In contrast, the single- and two-story wood-frame houses in the United States and the light wooden homes in Japan are some of the safest places to be during an earthquake. Although these buildings are not especially reinforced, their relatively lightweight design gives them more flexibility during a quake, and the debris is less likely to be heavy enough to crush someone in the event of a collapse.

Builders and scientists now take many precautions to ensure that buildings are safe during an earthquake. Many homes are now constructed so that their timber frames are bolted to the foundations. This prevents them from separating during an earthquake. Concrete reinforced with metal rods can withstand greater shocks than older, unreinforced structures.

The elasticity of a building—its ability to move and then return to its original shape—is very important. It may not seem possible that a building made of concrete and steel could be elastic, but many newer structures are built so that the walls and roof can withstand some shaking without damage. The key is to connect the walls and roof to the foundation to form a strong box. If the earth shakes, the whole structure will not fall apart. Although there may be damage, a collapse will not injure or kill anyone.

and injuries from an earthquake come from the damage or collapse of buildings. Most countries do not have building codes for constructing earthquake-resistant structures, and thousands may be killed when unsafe structures collapse during a quake. Miraculous rescues, such as the following news account from the earthquake that struck Gujarat, India, on January 26, 2001, underscore the danger of living in collapse-prone structures:

At least four people were found alive on Monday, including an eight-month-old boy in Bhuj [a village in India], and a seven-month-old girl dug from the rubble of her home in the nearby [Indian] town of Bhachau. In the case of the "miracle boy," as he is being called, doctors said the warmth of his dead mother's body helped him survive three days in the ruins of a collapsed building in Bhuj's Kansara Market. Rescuers had earlier pulled to safety a 90-year-old woman, apparently saved by a sewing machine which shielded her head from falling masonry. The baby girl was reunited with her delighted mother and father who had been outside their home when the earthquake struck. But much of the work was excavating the dead, and emergency workers point out that any more rescues will be nothing short of miraculous.[58]

In the United States, most cities have building codes that specify general safety measures that all buildings must have, including approved types of materials used in construction, the location of fire sprinklers, and the number and location of emergency stairwells, among other features. In earthquake-prone areas such as California, building codes include additional regulations for earthquake safety. For example, because an earthquake shakes the ground back and forth in a horizontal motion, buildings must be able to withstand that kind of movement.

To design structures that can withstand earthquakes, architects and engineers must understand how an earthquake causes stress on a building. In California, scientists and geologists have installed instruments—which measure how the building responds to ground movements beneath it—in structures throughout most earthquake-prone areas. Every time an earthquake shakes the building, scientists gather new information about the strength of the structure. One example of how these instruments helped improve building safety is recounted by a USGS scientist:

In 1984 the magnitude 6.2 Morgan Hill, California, earthquake shook the West Valley College campus, 20 miles away. Instruments in the college gymnasium showed that its roof was so flexible that in a stronger or closer earthquake the building might be severely damaged, threatening the safety of occupants. At that time, these flexible roof designs were permitted by the Uniform Building Code [a set of standards used in many states]. . . . In 1991, as a direct result of what was learned about the West Valley College gymnasium roof, the Uniform Building Code was revised. It now recommends that such roofs be made less flexible and therefore better able to withstand large nearby earthquakes.[59]

Today, hospitals, bridges, dams, aqueducts, and other public structures are fitted with instruments that measure their movement. Other earthquake-prone states that use the instruments include Illinois, South Carolina, New York, Tennessee, Idaho, Washington, Alaska, and Hawaii. The instruments themselves will do nothing to lessen the damage of an earthquake. But if severe tremors strike, scientists will have new information to help make the next generation of buildings safer.

The Transamerica Pyramid in San Francisco, designed to withstand an earthquake, stands next to a building which survived the 1906 earthquake.

The Problem of Older Buildings

Older structures, which were not built to modern building codes, are among the most dangerous places to be during an earthquake. Most building codes do not apply to structures already built and in use when the new rules are put into effect. This means that only new construction must be built according to the code's rules and regulations. It is usually time consuming and costly to retrofit older buildings; owners of older structures usually do not make changes or renovations to their structures, even if the structures do not conform to new regulations.

In some cases, this flaw in the building code has been instrumental in analyzing structures damaged during quakes. When older buildings are damaged in an earthquake, architects and seismologists can see firsthand how strong or weak specific design elements can be. For example, Long Beach, California, was hit by a large earthquake in 1933. Most of the damage from this quake was to older, unreinforced buildings, which at the time included many school buildings. Fortunately, the earthquake struck after 5 P.M., when children had already gone home for the day. However, if the quake had struck earlier, city officials estimated that many children would have been injured, or perhaps killed. As a result of the quake, builders and city planners were able to determine how and why the structures failed. Soon after, California legislators passed a law that added new earthquake codes to new school construction.

Public Buildings Must Be Extra Safe

Building codes require that a structure survive an earthquake without falling down or injuring people, but the codes do not dictate that it be usable afterward. Thus, many buildings that survive an initial shaking are later found to be uninhabitable and must be torn down. For this reason, it is very important that public structures be built strong enough to withstand an earthquake, and also to stay undamaged and operational after the quake is over.

It is generally accepted that if laws require citizens to be in a certain place at a certain time—such as children in school—then the government that imposes and enforces the requirement has a responsibility to keep people safe. For this reason, many public structures such as schools are constructed to remain safe even after a quake has hit. The same thinking goes for buildings such as hospitals, which are vital emergency resources in any disaster. Hospitals must remain open and operational to help the injured and the sick. However, people who design hospital buildings sometimes neglect other, vital elements that must also survive an earthquake. For example, a hospital must have electricity and running water, and access roads must be safely usable.

Failure to protect important infrastructure elements was brought to light by two damaging earthquakes in California, one in 1971 and another in 1994. After the 1971 San Fernando earthquake, four hospitals were severely damaged including the brand new Olive View Hospital, which had been built to meet the latest earthquake-

As a result of the damage to hospitals (like this one) in the 1971 San Fernando earthquake, new building codes were developed to make the buildings safer.

resistant building codes. During the earthquake, however, the first floor of one ward caved in completely, the main facility was heavily damaged, and two people died. Fortunately, the hospital was not operational and there were no patients in the building. Had the hospital been open, many deaths and injuries might have occured.

As a result of this disaster, new building codes were created that would make the hospital structures safer. But no one bothered to consider the lifelines to the hospital and how they would hold up in a quake. Ironically, the new Olive View Hospital, built in 1976, experienced intense shaking in the 1994 Northridge earthquake and survived completely. However, water mains inside the building broke from the strain, forcing the hospital to close at a time when it was most needed.

Each earthquake is a disaster. But every time an earthquake hits, scientists, engineers, architects, technicians, and other professionals in the field gather new information. This information may eventually help geologists predict the next earthquake. It also will assist city planners in making all structures safer when the next quake strikes.

Epilogue

Earthquakes, unlike other natural disasters such as hurricanes, tornadoes, or floods, strike without warning. Day or night, suddenly the ground begins to heave and roll. Objects on shelves tremble and crash to the ground. Buildings collapse. Then suddenly, usually less than a minute later, the shaking stops. Some areas are destroyed, while others seem untouched. Thousands are killed or injured, and thousands more become homeless. In one moment, their world changes forever.

But preparing for earthquakes is tricky at best, and sometimes futile. Most people tend to regard earthquakes as a remote danger that will likely never threaten them. Most people choose to ignore the threat, since it seems so unlikely that the power of a quake will touch their own lives. They will deal with it, they reason, if they are faced with it.

Yet the effects of an earthquake can be fast and deadly, unlike any other natural disaster. When storms, floods, or other disasters approach, people usually have enough warning to escape or to take precautionary measures. Even when a disaster causes great destruction, most people had some warning. This is not the case with earthquakes. No one can predict a quake. Scientists cannot determine how powerful a quake will be, where it will hit, how much damage it will do, or the other effects that will accompany it. Earthquakes catch people by deadly surprise.

This is the most frightening aspect of an earthquake—the element of surprise. No matter how well structures are built, how trained city organizations are to deal with a disaster, or how aware the citizens are of the threat, an earthquake always strikes without

This store in San Francisco carries a number of earthquake preparedness products.

warning. The power of an earthquake is unlike that of any other natural force in the world, and humans are helpless to stop it. All they can do is be aware of the danger and prepare with safety planning, earthquake-resistant structures, and awareness that it can, someday, happen to them.

Notes

Introduction

1. *National Geographic*, "Kobe Wakes to a Nightmare," July 1995, pp. 112–36.

2. *The January 17, 1995 Kobe Earthquake: An EQE Summary Report*, April 1995. www.eqe.com/publications/kobe/introduc.htm.

Chapter 1: Earthquakes in History

3. Quoted in Kerry Sieh and Simon LeVay, *The Earth in Turmoil*. New York: W. H. Freeman, 1998, pp. 205–206.

4. Philip L. Fradkin, *Magnitude 8*. Los Angeles: University of California Press, 1998, p. 25.

5. Quoted in Fradkin, *Magnitude 8*, p. 25.

6. Sieh and LeVay, *The Earth in Turmoil*, pp. 212–13.

7. Quoted in Sieh and LeVay, *The Earth in Turmoil*, p. 213.

8. Bruce A. Bolt, *Earthquakes and Geological Discovery*. New York: W. H. Freeman, 1993, p. 2.

9. Quoted in Sieh and LeVay, *The Earth in Turmoil*, p. 230.

10. Quoted in Sieh and LeVay, *The Earth in Turmoil*, p. 233.

11. Quoted in "Earthquake Myths and Folklore," Center for Earthquake Research and Information. www.ceri.memphis.edu/public/myths.shtml.

12. Quoted in "Earthquake Myths and Folklore."

13. Bolt, *Earthquakes and Geological Discovery*, p. 4.

14. Bolt, *Earthquakes and Geological Discovery*, p. 4.

15. Quoted in James M. Gere and Haresh C. Shah, *Terra Non Firma*. Stanford, CA: Stanford Alumni Association, 1984, p. 11.

16. Bolt, *Earthquakes and Geological Discovery*, pp. 5–6.

17. Bolt, *Earthquakes and Geological Discovery*, p. 6.

Chapter 2: What Causes Earthquakes?

18. John H. Hodgson, *Earthquakes and Earth Structure*. Englewood Cliffs, NJ: Prentice-Hall, 1964, pp. 10–11.

19. Sieh and LeVay, *The Earth in Turmoil*, p. 61.

20. Quoted in Fradkin, *Magnitude 8*, p. 100.

21. Sieh and LeVay, *The Earth in Turmoil*, p. 63.

22. Quoted in "This Dynamic Earth," U.S. Geological Survey publication. http://pubs.usgs.gov/publications/text/historical/html.

23. Sieh and LeVay, *The Earth in Turmoil*, p. 6.

24. Quoted in Sieh and LeVay, *The Earth in Turmoil*, p. 10.

25. Bruce A. Bolt, *Earthquakes*. New York: W. H. Freeman, 1993, p. 73.

26. Bolt, *Earthquakes and Geological Discovery*, pp. 76–77.

27. Alwyn Scarth, *Vulcan's Fury*. New Haven, CT: Yale University Press, 1999, pp. 127–28.

28. Gere and Shah, *Terra Non Firma*, p. 25.

Chapter 3: The Earth Moves

29. Quoted in Bolt, *Earthquakes and Geological Discovery*, p. 26.

30. Sieh and LeVay, *The Earth in Turmoil*, p. 120.

31. Quoted in Gere and Shah, *Terra Non Firma*, p. 69.

32. Ellen J. Prager, *Furious Earth*. New York: McGraw-Hill, 2000, pp. 46–47.

33. Prager, *Furious Earth*, p. 40.

34. D. S. Halacy Jr., *Earthquakes*. New York: Bobbs-Merrill, 1974, p. 48.

35. Gere and Shah, *Terra Non Firma*, p. 1.

36. Hodgson, *Earthquakes and Earth Structure*, p. 48.

37. Gere and Shah, *Terra Non Firma*, p. 2.

Chapter 4: After the Shock

38. Bolt, *Earthquakes*, p. 83.
39. Quoted in Bolt, *Earthquakes*, p. 87.
40. Gere and Shah, *Terra Non Firma*, pp. 30–31.
41. U.S. Geological Survey, National Landslide Information Center, "Second El Salvador earthquake causes additional landslides." http://landslides.usgs.gov/html_files/centrala1.shtml.
42. Gere and Shah, *Terra Non Firma*, p. 32.
43. Gere and Shah, *Terra Non Firma*, p. 32.
44. U.S. Geological Survey, Earthquakes Hazards Program, "Narrative of strong ground shaking and liquefaction on Harbor Island (south of downtown Seattle) during the Nisqually earthquake." www.geophys.washington.edu/SEIS/EQ_Special/WEBDIR_01022818543p/quakestory.html.
45. Bolt, *Earthquakes*, p. 165.
46. Sieh and LeVay, *The Earth in Turmoil*, p. 122.
47. Bolt, *Earthquakes*, p. 219.
48. Sieh and LeVay, *The Earth in Turmoil*, p. 121.
49. Gere and Shah, *Terra Non Firma*, p. 48.
50. Anne M. Rosenthal, "The Next Wave," *California Wild*, Spring 1999. www.calacademy.org/calwild/spring99/tsunamis.htm.

Chapter 5: Can We Predict Earthquakes?

51. Quoted in Halacy, *Earthquakes*, p. 122.
52. U.S. Geological Survey publication, "Predicting Earthquakes." http://pubs.usgs.gov/gip/earthq1/predict.html, p. 1.
53. Gere and Shah, *Terra Non Firma*, p. 102.
54. Bolt, *Earthquakes and Geological Discovery*, p. 191.
55. Prager, *Furious Earth*, p. 84.
56. Ruth Ludwin, "Earthquake Prediction Information," University of Washington Geophysics Program, Seismology

Lab, Seattle, Washington. www.geophys.washington.edu/
SEIS/PNSN/INFO_GENERAL/eq_prediction.html.

57. Prager, *Furious Earth*, p. 85.

58. "India Urges Faster Quake Help," Tuesday, January 30,
2001, BBC News website. http://news.bbc.co.uk/hi/english/
world/south_asia/ newsid_1143000/1143232.stm.

59. U.S. Geological Survey, "Building Safer Structures."
http://quake.wr.usgs.gov/prepare/factsheets/SaferStructures.

Glossary

body wave: A seismic wave that is created by an earthquake. Body waves travel through the interior of the earth. P waves and S waves are body waves.

continental drift: The theory that the earth's surface was once covered by one huge landmass. Pieces of the landmass split off and moved to form continents.

crust: The thin outer layer of the earth's surface.

earthquake: Shaking of the earth caused by a sudden movement of rock beneath its surface.

elastic rebound: Event in which rocks under extreme pressure suddenly break and return to their original position.

epicenter: That point on the earth's surface directly above the hypocenter, or focus, of an earthquake.

fault: A weak point, or rupture, in the earth's crust.

focus: The origin point of an earthquake deep within the earth.

hypocenter: The location of the focus of an earthquake.

intensity: A measure of the effects of an earthquake at a particular place on humans, structures, and the land.

liquefaction: A process during an earthquake in which soil and water join to form a quicksand-like material.

magnitude: A measure of the strength of an earthquake by the energy it releases.

P wave: Primary wave. P waves are the fastest body waves.

plate: One of the huge sections that make up the earth's crust.

plate tectonics: The theory that the earth's crust and upper mantle is broken into a number of moving plates.

reflect: To bounce back from a surface.

refract: To bend or change direction.

Richter scale: A system used to measure the strength of an earthquake.

S wave: Secondary wave. These waves move more slowly than P waves.

seismic: Having to do with earthquakes.

seismograph: An instrument that records the motions of the earth, especially earthquakes.

seismologist: A scientist who studies earthquakes.

subduction: The process in which one plate collides with and is forced down under another plate.

surface waves: Earthquake waves that move over the surface of the earth.

tsunami: A huge sea wave that is caused by an earthquake or other large-scale disturbance of the ocean floor.

For Further Reading

Mary Barnes, *More Freaky Facts About Natural Disasters.* New York: Aladdin Paperbacks, 2001. Vivid and fun accounts of strange and weird facts about earthquakes, volcanoes, fires, tsunamis, and landslides.

Bill Haduch, *Earthquake!* (Discovery Kids). New York: Dutton Books, 2000. This fun book—it shakes when you pull a string—is filled with information and facts about earthquakes.

Cristopher F. Lampton, *Earthquake* (A Disaster Book). New York: Millbrook Press, 1994. One in a series, this book gives clear, easy-to-digest information about earthquakes.

Lin Sutherland, *Earthquakes and Volcanoes.* Reader's Digest Pathfinders. Pleasantville, NY: Reader's Digest, 2000. This over-sized, colorful book explains the general ideas about earthquakes and volcanoes and why they occur.

Works Consulted

Books

Bruce A. Bolt, *Earthquakes*. New York: W. H. Freeman, 1993. A comprehensive and easy-to-understand account of earthquakes and their causes.

Bruce A. Bolt, *Earthquakes and Geological Discovery*. New York: W. H. Freeman, 1993. Bolt presents scientific information about earthquakes and seismology in a simple and easy-to-read format.

Philip L. Fradkin, *Magnitude 8*. Los Angeles: University of California Press, 1998. The author studied the San Andreas Fault and used his knowledge to write an account of past and recent earthquakes. He also speculates what will happen in the event of a magnitude 8 earthquake in heavily populated southern California.

James M. Gere and Haresh C. Shah, *Terra Non Firma*. Stanford, CA: Stanford Alumni Association, 1984. The authors, respected scientists, give an informative, firsthand account of earthquake study.

D. S. Halacy Jr., *Earthquakes*. Indianapolis and New York: Bobbs-Merrill, 1974. This book is a comprehensive overview of earthquake history and study.

John H. Hodgson, *Earthquakes and Earth Structure*. Englewood Cliffs, NJ: Prentice-Hall, 1964. This book focuses on the geology of earthquakes and their origins.

Ellen J. Prager, *Furious Earth*. New York: McGraw-Hill, 2000. Prager includes many natural disasters, including volcanoes, earthquakes, and tsunamis in her easy-to-read book.

Andrew Robinson, *Earthshock*. London: Thames and Hudson, 1993. This book, an overview of the various kinds of natural disasters, includes a chapter about earthquakes.

Alwyn Scarth, *Vulcan's Fury*. New Haven, CT: Yale University Press, 1999. Scarth presents a comprehensive look at volcanoes and the efforts to combat their destructive forces.

Kerry Sieh and Simon LeVay, *The Earth in Turmoil*. New York: W. H. Freeman, 1998. Sieh and LeVay examine the effects of earthquake and volcanic activity around the world.

Periodical

National Geographic, "Kobe Wakes to a Nightmare," July 1995.

Internet Sources

Center for Earthquake Research and Information, "Earthquake Myths and Folklore." www.ceri.memphis.edu/public/myths.shtml.

Department of Geological Engineering and Sciences, Michigan Technological University. www.geo.mtu.edu/UPSeis/waves.html.

"India Urges Faster Quake Help," January 30, 2001, BBC News website.http://news.bbc.co.uk/hi/english/world/south_asia/newsid _1143000/1143232.stm.

The January 17, 1995 Kobe Earthquake: An EQE Summary Report, April 1995. www.eqe.com/publication/kobe/introduc.htm.

Ruth Ludwin, "Earthquake Prediction Information," University of Washington Geophysics Program, Seismology Lab, Seattle, Washington. www.geophys.washington.edu/SEIS/PNSN/INFO_ GENERAL/eq_prediction.html.

John Muir, "The Earthquake." www.sierraclub.org/johnmuirexhibit/ writings/theearthquake.html.

The Nevada Seismological Laboratory, University of Nevada. www.seismo.unr.edu/ftp/pub/louie/class/100/effects-kobe.html.

The Nevada Seismological Laboratory, University of Nevada. www.seismo.unr.edu/ftp/pub/louie/class/100/seismic-waves.html.

Anne M. Rosenthal, "The Next Wave," *California Wild*, Spring 1999. www.calacademy.org/calwild/spring99/tsunamis.htm.

SLO County Office of Emergency Services: The Parkfield Earthquake Prediction Experiment. www.slonet.org/vv/ipoes/oespark.html#predict.

U.S. Geological Survey, "Building Safer Structures." http://quake.wr.usgs.gov/prepare/factsheets/SaferStructures.

U.S. Geological Survey, Earthquake Hazards Program, "Narrative of strong ground shaking and liquefaction on Harbor Island (south of downtown Seattle) during the Nisqually earthquake." www.geophys.washington.edu/SEIS/EQ_Special/WEBDIR_01022818543p/quakestory.html.

U.S. Geological Survey, Earthquake Hazards Program—Northern California, "1906 Marked the Dawn of the Scientific Revolution." http://quake.wr.usgs.gov/info/1906/revolution.html.

U.S. Geological Survey, Earthquake Hazards Program—Northern California, "Reid's Elastic Rebound Theory." http://quake.wr.usgs.gov/info/1906/reid.html.

U.S. Geological Survey, "Earthquakes in History." http://pubs.usgs.gov/gip/earthq1/history.html.

U.S. Geological Survey, "How Earthquakes Happen." http://pubs.usgs.gov/gip/earthq1/how.html.

U.S. Geological Survey, "Measuring Earthquakes." http://pubs.usgs.gov/gip/earthq1/measure.html.

U.S. Geological Survey, National Landslide Information Center, "Second El Salvador earthquake causes additional landslides." http://landslides.usgs.gov/html_files/centrala1.shtml.

U.S. Geological Survey, "NEIC: Seismographs—Keeping Track of Earthquakes." http://pubs.usgs.gov/neis/seismology/keeping_track.html.

U.S. Geological Survey, "Predicting Earthquakes." http://pubs.usgs.gov/gip/earthq1/predict.html.

U.S. Geological Survey, "Reducing Earthquake Losses Throughout the United States." http://quake.wr.usgs.gov/prepare/factsheets/Pac NW.

U.S. Geological Survey, "The Severity of an Earthquake." http:// pubs.usgs.gov/earthq4/severitygip.html.

U.S. Geological Survey, "Speeding Earthquake Disaster Relief." http://quake.wr.usgs.gov/prepare/factsheets/Mitigation.

U.S. Geological Survey, "This Dynamic Earth." http://pubs.usgs. gov/publications/text/historical/html.

U.S. Geological Survey, "Where Earthquakes Occur." http://pubs. usgs.gov/gip/earthq1/where.html.

Website

U.S. Geological Survey. www.usgs.gov.

Index

Picture Credits

Cover Photo: S. Mango/Photo Researchers, Inc.

Associated Press, 50, 53, 65, 66, 71, 85, 86, 93

Associated Press, NASA/JPL/NIMA, 33

© Bettmann/CORBIS, 41, 52, 70, 76

© Jonathan Blair/CORBIS, 82

© Lloyd Cluff/CORBIS, 35, 55, 69, 81, 91

© CORBIS, 10, 11

© Raymond Gehman/CORBIS, 14

© Historical Picture Archive/CORBIS, 19

Hulton/Archive by Getty Images, 13, 21, 22, 24, 28, 39, 89

Hulton-Deutsch Collection/CORBIS, 74

Chris Jouan, 31, 34, 36, 44, 46

© Layne Kennedy/CORBIS, 83

© Daniel Lainé/CORBIS, 17

Library of Congress, 27

© Roger Ressmeyer/CORBIS, 61, 79

© Reuters NewMedia Inc./CORBIS, 63

© Vince Streano/CORBIS, 47

© David & Peter Turnley/CORBIS, 57

© Michael S. Yamashita/CORBIS, 9, 59

About the Author

Award-winning children's magazine editor and writer Allison Lassieur has published more than two dozen books about history, world cultures, and health. A writer for magazines such as *National Geographic World, Highlights for Children, Scholastic News,* and *Disney Adventures,* she also writes novels, puzzle books, and computer game materials. In addition to writing, Ms. Lassieur studies medieval history. She lives and works in Pennsylvania.